LINCOLN CHRISTIAN UNIVERSITY

D1491156

101 More
Great Games for
Kids

101 More Great Games for KIDS

Active, Bible-based Fun for Christian Education

Jolene L. Roehlkepartain

Abingdon Press

Nashville

101 MORE GREAT GAMES FOR KIDS
ACTIVE, BIBLE-BASED FUN FOR CHRISTIAN EDUCATION

Copyright © 2007 by Abingdon Press

All rights reserved.
No part of this work may be reproduced or transmitted in any form or by any means, electronic or mechanical, including photocopying and recording, or by any information storage or retrieval system, except as may be expressly permitted by the 1976 Copyright Act or in writing from the publisher. Requests for permission should be addressed to Abingdon Press, P.O. Box 801, 201 Eighth Avenue South, Nashville, TN 37202-0801 or permissions@abingdonpress.com.

This book is printed on acid-free paper.

Library of Congress Cataloging-in-Publication Data

Roehlkepartain, Jolene L.
 101 more great games for kids : active, Bible-based fun for Christian education / Jolene L. Roehlkepartain.
  p. cm.
 Includes index.
 ISBN-13: 978-0-687-33407-0 (pbk. : alk. paper)
 1. Games in Christian education. 2. Church work with children. I. Title. II. Title: One hundred and one more great games for kids. III. Title: One hundred one more great games for kids.

 BV1536.3.R65 2000
 268'.432—dc22

                                                                 2006016141

All scripture quotations unless noted otherwise are taken from the *New Revised Standard Version of the Bible*, copyright 1989 by the Division of Christian Education of the National Council of the Churches of Christ in the United States of America. Used by permission. All rights reserved.

07 08 09 10 11 12 13 14 15 16—10 9 8 7 6 5 4 3 2 1
MANUFACTURED IN THE UNITED STATES OF AMERICA

To Linnea

For always inspiring me to play more—
and to have more fun

1519

126999

PPP∂6|

Contents

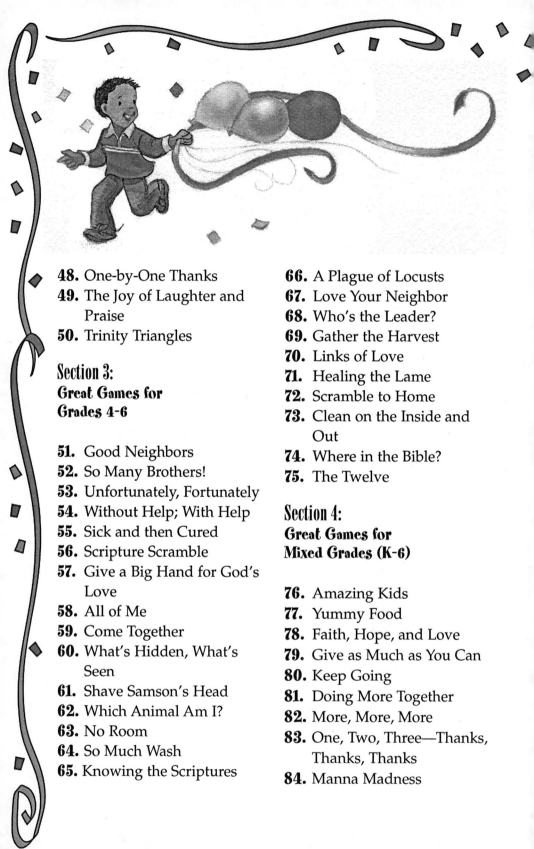

Ten Keys to Making Great Games Even Better

Looking for More Great Games?

Scripture Index

Topical Index

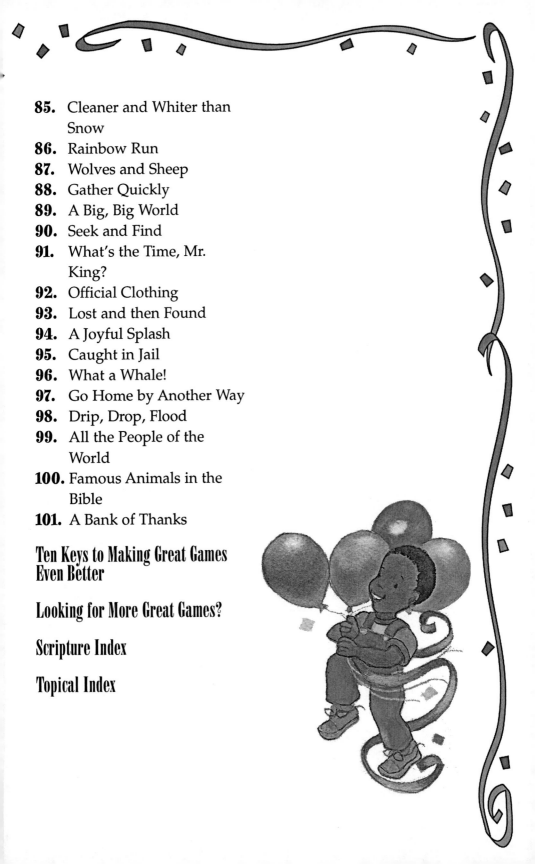

Introduction

Learning More Through Play

Tug. Yank. Pull.

I glanced down. There was Thomas, tugging at my shirt.

"Are you ready to play?" Thomas asked.

"After worship," I said as people started getting into place for the service to begin. Thomas grinned and clapped his hands.

During the education hour following worship, I taught Thomas and the rest of my Sunday school class. The kids know that when Jolene teaches, you don't sit still and learn. You get up and move. You get up and play. That's why Thomas had sought me out before worship. He came to church ready to play.

At the end of the education hour, I asked the children what they learned about the Bible story. Thomas knew. So did the rest of the kids. They knew because they not only heard the lesson, they experienced it. They learned because they played.

Children—whether they're four, eight, or twelve don't do well when they sit too long. In fact, their minds often follow what their bodies are doing. When you get children's bodies moving, you're more likely to get their minds jumping as well.

When we're playing games during our Sunday school lesson, a lot more is happening than what you can see:

- **Kids are learning more about scripture**—Each of the 101 games in this book tie into a scripture passage. As children play the game, they're also expanding their biblical literacy.
- **Kids are getting to know each other better**—Most of our education classes have children who live in different communities and attend different schools. We have to work hard to help them get to know each other and to develop friendships. Kids "who have a best friend at church are 21 percent more likely to report attending church at least once a week and 26 percent more likely to report having a strong, more active faith," says Michael D. Lindsay, Sociology Research Affiliate at Princeton University (as quoted in a Group news release May 20, 2005). Playing games can help children build community.
- **Kids are excited to come**—Ask any parent how easy it is to get their children to go to education classes at your church. If kids are stimulated, having fun, and know each other, they want to come. Stimulating, fun games that build community can be a big draw for children.
- **Kids are learning more**—Howard Gardner's theory on multiple intelligences (also known as the seven learning styles) says that children learn more when we teach by more than one learning style. The games in this book tap into all seven learning styles: linguistic (words and language), logical-mathematical (logic and mathematics), musical, bodily-kinesthetic (body movement), spatial-visual (images and space), interpersonal (other people's feelings), and intrapersonal (self-awareness). (See www.businessballs.com, © Howard Gardner's Multiple Intelligences concept; review, remaining material, design, and code Alan Chapman 1995-2006.) Some games tap into two learning styles at a time, others incorporate much more.
- **Kids are growing in faith**—Search Institute researchers found that "the *way Christian education is done* matters as much as, if not more than, any other area of congregational life" (p. 56). In the Search Institute report *Effective Christian Education: A*

National Study of Protestant Congregations, researchers discovered that young people who are involved in strong Christian education programs are more likely to grow spiritually.

"Christian education matters much more than we expected," say Search Institute researchers. "Of all the areas of congregational life we examined, involvement in an effective Christian education program has the strongest tie to a person's growth in faith and to loyalty to one's congregation and denomination. While other congregational factors also matter, nothing matters more than effective Christian education" (p. 2). (Benson, Peter L., & Eklin, Carolyn H. (1990). *Effective Christian education: A national study of Protestant congregations—A summary report on faith, loyalty, and congregational life.* Minneapolis: Search Institute.)

To me, an effective Christian education means engaging children in ways that help them learn and grow in faith. Playing games with children—meaningful, stimulating games based on scripture and Christian principles—helps children to grow spiritually. When I see children excited and giggling during games, I know they're learning. I can think of no better way to teach children than by playing games that make all of our faith journeys more meaningful and fun.

Great Games for PRESCHOOLERS

When I was a child, we had a pet rabbit that had ten babies. When the babies' eyes opened, my sister and I took out all the babies and let them loose in the backyard.

Chaos ensued. Bunnies hopped everywhere. Eventually our parents came out and helped us round up the bunnies, and after that, we took them out one at a time.

Playing games with preschoolers often can feel like having ten bunnies running around. Chaos happens more often than order. Some people refuse to play games with preschoolers because they say it can't be done.

Yet, preschoolers need to move. They need to play, and even though games can become chaotic at times, it's always worth playing with this age group. Yes, at first games will seem out of control, but over time, preschoolers will get the hang of playing together.

Although playing games with preschoolers means tolerating unpredictability, I'm always surprised when most of the pre-schoolers catch on to what's going on. I've overhead four-year-olds tell their moms how much fun they had playing games and what they learned—when the four year old had spent a lot of the time hiding under the table.

I've learned to become patient and to trust in the mystery with playing games with preschoolers. In fact, if you ask me which age group I prefer to teach, I always pick preschoolers. Even though lessons and games get messy, I find great joy in their insights and their enthusiasm. Recently when we were playing a game about Noah's Ark, one boy said, "That ark must have been bigger than the zoo! I wish I could have seen that ark." During another lesson about creation, a girl said, "If it took seven days to make the world, God must have worked very long days—just like my Daddy."

It's delightful when preschoolers discover that God's love "is bigger than the whole world" and that helping others "is the bestest thing we can do."

Try the following twenty-five games with your preschoolers. All are different, and all emphasize a fun way for preschoolers to learn more about God—and themselves. As they play, preschoolers experience the wonders of God's word and God's world.

That's something I'm thrilled to witness every time I teach.

On Our Way

Scripture: Joseph and Mary travel from Nazareth to Bethlehem, and shepherds and wise men travel to see the baby. (Luke 2:1-20 and Matthew 2:1-12)

This Game Teaches: People traveled a long way to see Jesus.

Materials: Five pieces of different-colored construction paper, marker

Game: Before the game, write one of each of these alphabet letters on a separate piece of construction paper. (If possible, try to use a yellow piece for the letter S.) The letters to write are: B, E, F, N, and S. Spread out the five pieces of paper throughout the room and clear the area in between.

Explain that you're going to play a travel game about Jesus' birth. Say that people came from long distances to see baby Jesus. Point out the five pieces of construction paper with the five letters on them. Ask the children to name the letters aloud. (This will help the preschoolers who may not recognize some of the letters.)

Say, "When I say a letter, run to the paper that has that letter on it. Stand on the letter or stand as close as you can. It will be very crowded, so stick close together. Then listen closely because I will name another letter, which you will then have to run to."

Tell the travel story:

- Mary was going to have a baby. She and Joseph lived in N for Nazareth. *(Pause while the children run to the letter N).*
- While they were in Nazareth, they heard that everyone needed to register in their hometown. So Mary and Joseph got on a donkey and went to B for Bethlehem. *(Pause.)*
- In Bethlehem, Jesus was born. Meanwhile, shepherds were in the F for fields. *(Pause.)* They were watching their sheep.
- They then saw angels in the S for sky. *(Pause.)*
- The shepherds were afraid in their F for fields. *(Pause.)*
- They were told not to be afraid by the angels in the S for sky. *(Pause.)*
- The angels told them to go to B for Bethlehem. *(Pause.)*
- In Bethlehem, the shepherds saw the baby Jesus. Meanwhile wise men were in the E for east. *(Pause.)*
- The wise men saw a bright star in the S for sky. *(Pause.)*
- The wise men followed the star to B for Bethlehem. *(Pause.)* There they saw Jesus.

End the game by saying, "Everyone traveled so far to see the birth of Jesus. They went from N for Nazareth. *(Pause.)* Wise men traveled from the E for east. *(Pause.)* Shepherds came from the F for fields. *(Pause.)* They all saw the star in the S for sky. *(Pause.)* They all came to B for Bethlehem."

Bonus Idea

Turn over the five pieces of colored paper and write one of these letters on each: C, H, N, P, and S. Have the children repeat the game, but use examples of the places they travel to and from in their own lives. Have C mean church, H mean home, N mean neighborhood, P mean preschool, and S mean store.

Roaring and Mooing: Two by Two

Scripture: The animals board the ark two by two. (Genesis 7)
This Game Teaches: God asked Noah to build an ark large enough to hold two of every animal.
Materials: None

Game: Ask children to line up two by two in a single line. Say, "God asked Noah to build a very big boat called an ark. This boat was so big that it could hold two of every animal."

Explain that everyone is going to pretend that they're animals marching toward the ark. Before you start, however, say that you will name an animal and then everyone will begin walking like that animal and making noises like that animal.

Name animals such as these (one at a time):

- Monkeys
- Horses
- Elephants
- Mice
- Dogs
- Cows
- Donkeys
- Cats
- Lions

Bonus Idea

Ask the children for additional animal ideas. Don't be surprised if you find the ark also had dinosaurs, hamsters, and ants. Preschoolers enjoy coming up with animals to mimic.

Right Versus Wrong

Scripture: Do what's right. (Psalm 119)
This Game Teaches: It's good to do the right thing instead of the wrong thing.
Materials: None

3

Game: Say, "God wants us to do the right thing, but sometimes we do the wrong thing. We're going to play a game about opposites."

Have the children stand. Say each statement and lead children in the actions that are in italics. Pause after each word in italics so that you can do the action.

- God wants us to walk *forward,* but sometimes we walk *backward.*
- God wants us to *smile,* but sometimes we *frown.*
- God wants us to *dance,* but sometimes we *cross our arms and won't move.*
- God wants us to go to the *right,* but sometimes we go to the *left.*
- God wants us to *look up,* but sometimes we *look down.*
- God wants us to *clap,* but sometimes we make *angry faces and boo.*
- God wants us to *move fast,* but sometimes we *go slow.*
- God wants us to *stand up,* but sometimes we *sit down.*

End the game by saying, "God wants us to do the right thing. Sometimes we do the wrong thing, and we need to do the opposite and do the right thing."

Pass On the Good News

Scripture: Tell the good news. (Matthew 28:19-20)
This Game Teaches: We can tell others the good news about God.
Materials: A straw for each child, one paper cup

4

Game: Have children sit in a circle. Give each child a straw. Read aloud Matthew 28:19-20.

Say, "We're going to pass on the good news in our circle. I have a paper cup." Place the paper cup upside down onto your straw. (It will wobble, but it won't fall off unless you really swing around the straw.) Explain that you're going to start passing the cup around the circle with your straw. The next child will insert his or her straw into the cup (along with your straw,) and then you will remove your straw. As you do this, say, "God loves you." Encourage children to continue going around the circle. As they pass along the cup, have them say, "God loves you."

After you go around the circle, do the game again with another piece of good news. Consider using these phrases one at a time:

- Jesus died for you.
- Our church is a great place.
- God is always with us.
- I like coming to church.

End the game by saying, "We passed along the good news! It's great that God loves us and that Jesus died for our sins."

Bonus Idea

If you have a lot of younger preschoolers, cut out the bottom of the cup. Do not use straws. Instead use the cup like a megaphone to tell the good news around the circle. With older children, adapt the game by using a thimble instead of a paper cup.

Food, Glorious Food

Scripture: After Solomon finishes building the temple and a palace, the people celebrate by having a great feast. (2 Chronicles 8)
This Game Teaches: We can celebrate after we work hard.
Materials: None

Game: Say, "In the Bible, God's people worked hard to do good things. In 2 Chronicles 8, it took the people twenty years to build a church and a castle. Afterward they celebrated by having a great feast with a lot of good food."

Ask the children to spread out throughout the playing area. Explain that you're going to name a food and you want the children to use their imagination and act like that food.

Name foods such as these (one at a time):
- Bread rising in an oven
- An orange being squeezed into juice
- Popcorn popping
- Grapes being washed
- A can of soda pop being opened
- Spaghetti noodles right out of the box
- Spaghetti noodles being cooked
- A sandwich (find two other children and make a sandwich)
- Melting ice cream
- Each child is a different ingredient in a cake, and they all need to come together to be stirred

End the game by saying, "There are many feasts in the Bible. It's good to celebrate and eat together."

Helpful Friends

Scripture: Friends lower a paralyzed man through a roof so Jesus can heal him. (Mark 2:1-12)
This Game Teaches: We can help others.
Materials: Blanket, toilet paper, bandages

6

Game: Before the game, set up one area to spread out a blanket, toilet paper, and bandages. Clear another area for a child to lie down. Make sure the area between the two areas is easy to maneuver through.

Ask for a volunteer. The volunteer will be the paralyzed man. Have the volunteer lie on the floor face up.

Explain that you and all the other children are the paralyzed man's friends. Surround the child lying on the floor. Have one child be at the person's head, another at the shoulders, another at the body, and two at the feet. If you have more children, have them give their support with the shoulders and body. Your position is to be near the body to lend the most support and monitor the preschoolers as they carry the child across the room.

Briefly tell the story of the friends carrying the paralyzed man to Jesus. Have all the children bend over or squat down into position. Explain that when you say go, the children are to lift the child gently and together you'll carry the child across the room.

Together gently carry the child across the room to the other area. Gently place the child onto the blanket. Tell the children that this man cannot walk. Ask what they could do with the toilet paper and bandages. Children may wrap the child's legs in toilet paper, as if they were using large bandages, to make the legs look like they're in a cast. They may place bandages over the parts where they think the child is wounded.

End the game by saying, "Jesus healed the paralyzed man, but Jesus could not have helped the man if the man's friends hadn't helped him first. It's good to help each other."

God Created the Four Seasons ... and More

Scripture: God created the earth and everything in it. (Genesis 1)

This Game Teaches: God created a lot of things we take for granted.

Materials: None

Game: Have the children sit in a circle. They can sit either on the floor or in chairs.

Talk about how God created the earth and everything in it. Explain that the children are to use their imaginations to pass an imaginary ball around the circle.

Pretend you have an imaginary ball, and you're passing it to the child on your right. Have the children pretend that they get the imaginary ball one at a time and pass it around the circle to the right.

When you receive the imaginary ball, begin to talk about how the ball is changing and that the children need to handle it according to what it's like. About every four or five children, change something about the imaginary ball. Use examples such as these:

- The ball is ice in winter.
- The ball is scorching hot in summer.
- The ball is wet in spring.
- The ball is covered with leaves in fall.
- The ball is huge.

- The ball is tiny and easy to lose.
- The ball is heavy.
- The ball is light.
- The ball is sticky.
- The ball is slimy.
- The ball is easy to drop.
- The ball moves fast.

End the game by saying, "God created everything. God created the four seasons and everything on earth. God also created our imaginations, which you used very well today."

The Gift of Love

Scripture: God loves us. (Romans 5:1-11)
This Game Teaches: God loves every single person.
Materials: A red paper heart for each child, black marker, a box that will hold the paper hearts and can be wrapped, two different kinds of inexpensive wrapping paper, and transparent tape

Game: Before you play this game, make a small red paper heart for each child. (Make a couple more than you expect to use.) On each heart write, God loves you. Place the hearts in a box and wrap the box with wrapping paper. Then wrap the box again (over the first layer of wrapping paper) with a different kind of wrapping paper. Wrap the box 10 to 12 times using alternating paper.

Have the children sit in a circle. Say that you have a present that holds a gift from God. Hand the gift to one child and ask the child to unwrap the first layer of wrapping paper.

When the child gets to the second layer, stop the child. Say, "More wrapping paper! I wonder what's inside?" Shake the box. "I've heard that there is a present for each one of you." Give the next child the box and ask him or her to unwrap one layer.

Continue around the circle. Ask each child to unwrap one layer of wrapping paper. As the children do so, ask them what they think God would put in a box. Say that you've never received a gift from God that you could hold.

End the game by having the last child open the box once it's unwrapped. Have the child give each child a heart. Say, "God loves you. What a great gift!"

8

Bonus Idea

Create paper hearts with the name of each one of the children. (Write one name per heart.) Place these hearts in between the layers of wrapping paper. As children get to a heart, ask what they have found. Read aloud the name. Acknowledge the child if he or she is present. Tape each heart with masking tape onto a wall and talk about how you love each child. By the time the box is unwrapped, you should have the entire class in a cluster of hearts on your wall.

Walk in Jesus' Steps

Scripture: Jesus calls; people follow. Jesus (John 8:12)
This Game Teaches: It's good to follow Jesus.
Materials: None

Game: Say, "In the Bible, Jesus called people to follow him. He said people who followed him would walk in the light and never in the dark."

Tell the children that you're going to play a walking game. Say that you're the leader and that children should walk in the exact way that you walk.

Start walking around the room. Then walk in these ways (one at a time):

- Tiptoe
- Walk fast
- Stomp
- Walk sideways
- Walk stiffly—as if your legs and arms were made of metal
- Walk on the outsides of your feet
- Walk backwards
- March
- Walk in a silly way
- Walk like a limp rag doll
- Walk in slow motion

End the game by saying, "You're great at following the leader. Jesus wants us to follow him and walk in the light."

God's Spies

Scripture: Spies explore the land of Canaan. (Numbers 13)
This Game Teaches: Sometimes you need to be sneaky to do God's work.
Materials: None

10

Game: Briefly tell the story from Numbers 13 about God needing spies to explore the land of Canaan.

Say, "We're going to be spies today. When I tell you to go, begin tiptoeing around the room like you're a spy. When I say, 'Quick, hide!' find a hiding place. Go into that place and be very quiet. When I say, 'It's safe to sneak,' come out and begin tiptoeing around the room again like a spy."

Play the game. Preschoolers love using their imagination, and many will become quite creative in their hiding and sneaking.

End the game by having one child be the leader and the other children follow him or her around the room. Have the child lead in sneaky, spy-like ways while the other children mimic his or her actions.

Hunt for the Cross

Scripture: Jesus was killed on a cross. (John 19:16-27)
This Game Teaches: The cross is an important symbol of our faith.
Materials: A hand-held cross

Game: Have children sit in a circle. Ask for a volunteer. Have the volunteer sit in the middle. Hand the volunteer a cross.

Say, "Jesus was killed on a cross. We have a cross in our church to remind us that Jesus died for our sins."

Explain that you're going to play a game. The child in the middle will hand the cross to one of the children in the circle. The child in the middle then covers his or her eyes with his or her hands while the children start passing the cross around the circle behind their backs.

At one point, say, "Stop! Shhhh." Remind the children to keep their hands behind their backs and to be quiet. Have the child in the middle open his or her eyes and then guess who is holding the cross. Let the child have two guesses. If he or she is right, he or she can be in the middle again. Otherwise, the child holding the cross gets to be in the middle. Play the game again.

End the game by placing the cross in the middle of the circle. Pray, "Thank you, Jesus, for dying on the cross for our sins. Amen."

11

Thankful Bounce

Scripture: Give thanks to God. (Psalm 75)
This Game Teaches: We have much to be thankful for.
Materials: An old sheet, three to four ping-pong balls

12

Game: Clear a playing area. Have the children form a circle and hold a sheet so that it's like a parachute. Say, "Psalm 75 says we should give thanks to God. I'm going to add a ping-pong ball to our sheet, and then we'll go around the circle and say one thing we're thankful for while we bounce the ping-pong ball up and down while slightly raising and lowering the sheet."

If preschoolers have never done this before, first have them practice moving the sheet to move the ping-pong ball. Once they get the hang of it, go around the circle and have each child name something he or she is thankful for.

Then add another ball. Go around the circle again and name something else you're thankful for. Continue doing this until all the ping-pong balls are bouncing on the sheet.

End the game by having the children come close together so that the middle of the sheet drops to the floor with the ping-pong balls

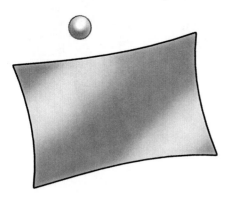

inside. Take the sheet and swing it over your shoulder like a sack. With the children still standing in a circle, together say, "Thank you, God!" as you lift your arms into the air.

Hidden Coins

Scripture: The lost coin. (Luke 15:8-10)
This Game Teaches: When you lose something, look for it. When you find it, rejoice.
Materials: Fifty pennies

Game: Before you play the game, hide fifty pennies around the room. Hide them so that preschoolers can easily find them.

Say, "The Bible tells the story about the lost coin. A woman lost her coin, and she looked and looked for it. When she found it, she celebrated. We're going to look for the lost coin. In this room there are fifty lost coins. When you find a coin, pick it up and say, 'I found it! I found it!' then keep looking for other coins. Ready? Let's play."

Play the game. When all the coins have been found (or most of them have), stop the game.

End the game by having the children keep their coins. (If a child or two didn't find any coins, ask if any of the children would like to share their coins. Most preschoolers are generous and don't like to have anyone left out.) Say, "We are sad when we lose things. We are happy when we find things. We can be happy that the lost coins have been found."

13

Bonus Idea

Instead of letting the children keep the pennies, consider passing around an offering plate and having each child keep one penny and place the rest in the offering plate.

A Rainbow of Color

Scripture: God sent a rainbow as a covenant. (Genesis 9:1-17)
This Game Teaches: God created a rainbow of beautiful colors.
Materials: Balloons in red, orange, yellow, green, blue, and purple
(enough so that each child can have one)

14

Game: Inflate balloons before you play the game. Make sure
each child gets one balloon, and distribute the balloons in this
order: red, orange, yellow, green, blue, and purple. Then start
over. For example, if you have ten children, you will have
distributed two reds, two oranges, two yellows, two greens,
one blue, and one purple.

Have the children spread out on a playing area while holding
their balloons. Have them sit down.

Say, "After the flood in the Bible, God gave a rainbow as a
promise that God would never flood the earth again. A rainbow has
six colors. When I name your color, jump up."

Say the six colors, one at a time: red,
orange, yellow, green, blue, and purple.
Then have the children sit down again.

Say, "I'm going to sing a song. When
you hear your color named, jump up."

Sing this song to the tune of *The
Farmer in the Dell*:

> The reds will now jump up
> The reds will now jump up.
> Heigh-ho the derry-oh,
> The reds will now jump up.

All the children holding red balloons
should now be standing. Ask them to sit
down. Sing the song again, but substitute
one of the other five colors for the color

red. Sing the song a total of six times so that each child gets to jump up once.

End the game by singing the song one more time. This time sing the word "rainbow" instead of an individual color. Have all the children jump up.

Bonus Idea

If your children have a lot of energy to burn, use the balloons to play another game. Have the children jog around the room with their balloons. Occasionally yell out a color. Any child with that color balloon should hold up his or her balloon over his or her head as he or she jogs. Be creative. Sometimes name two or three colors at a time.

A Crowning Achievement

Scripture: When you obey and help out, the wisdom you receive will be your crown. (Proverbs 4:1-9)

This Game Teaches: Be responsible and help.

Materials: Find a place (or area) that needs cleaning up. This place could be in your room or somewhere within your church.
Optional: Create yellow construction paper crowns for the children to wear after the game

15

Game: Before you play this game, find a place or area that needs cleaning up. Maybe the church nursery has toys strewn all over. Maybe an area outside of your church has a bunch of litter. Maybe you have a toy or book area in your room that's a mess. Choose one area where preschoolers can help clean it up.

Gather in the place that is in disarray. Say, "Sometimes places get to be a mess. Who can tell me where they have been lately that has been messy?" Some children will say their bedroom. Others will name a closet, hallway, or other area of their house.

Say, "The Bible says that it's good to listen to Moms, Dads, and other adults. When we do what they tell us, the Bible says you will live a good life. Who sees a messy area near here?" Let one of the children point out the messy area near you.

Say, "Together, let's clean it up. Ready? Let's get started." Encourage everyone to participate, and clean up the area with the children.

Optional: If you created yellow construction paper crowns, crown each child afterward.

End the game by having the children form a circle or half circle around the cleaned-up area. Say, "I'm proud of each one of you for listening and helping to clean this up." Then go around to each child and place your hand on his or her head while saying, "(_Name of child_), I crown you the most Honorable Cleaner Upper."

So Much to Be Thankful For

Scripture: Give thanks to God. (Psalm 107:1-9)
This Game Teaches: To name what we're thankful for.
Materials: None

Game: Have the children sit in a wide circle (so that there is plenty of space between each child). Say, "God gives us many great things to be thankful for. We're going to play a thank-you game. We'll go around the circle. When it's your turn, jump up and yell one thing you're thankful for."

16

Go around the circle and have each child name something while jumping up. (After they jump up, have them sit back down.)

After you go around the circle once, repeat the game but see if the children can go faster—jumping and naming something they're thankful for.

If the children ever get stuck for ideas, remind them to think of animals, foods, toys, colors, and people.

End the game by having the children jump up at the same time and shout, "Thank you, God, for everything!"

A Pile of Rocks

Scripture: A pile of rocks shows the agreement between Jacob and Laban. (Genesis 31:45-49)

This Game Teaches: Ordinary objects can become powerful symbols.

Materials: A rock for each child (ideally try to find about a two-inch diameter rock for each child), a piece of chalk for each child

17

Game: Give each child a rock and a piece of chalk. Say, "We're going to do an activity with rocks." Encourage children to draw a picture or color their rock with chalk. Before they start, encourage them to decide what to do before they start. For example, they could completely color their rock, they could draw the lines and cracks that are already in the rock, or they could draw a picture.

Let the children draw or color their rocks with chalk. When they finish, ask each one to tell the group about what they did and why.

Then have children form a circle and hold their rocks. Say, "In the Bible, people often made a pile of rocks as an altar. Let's make an altar now with our rocks." Have each child (one at a time) add his or her rock to the middle of your circle.

End the activity by having children fold their hands in prayer, bow their heads, and close their eyes. Pray, "Thank you, God, for the rocks you give us. Thank you for giving us talent to draw and color. Thank you for your altar where we can come to you. Amen."

Terrific Trees

Scripture: A healthy tree bears good fruit. (Luke 6:43-45)
This Game Teaches: Do the right thing.
Materials: An area outside with trees (either on your church grounds or at a nearby park)

Game: Gather around a tree (either on your church grounds or at a nearby park). Say, "God made lots of trees. What do you know about trees?" Let children respond.

Say, "The Bible says we can make good choices and help others—even trees. Let's sing a song while we play this game with our tree."

Have the children form a circle around the tree. Sing this song together to the tune of *Are You Sleeping?* (Or you also may know the song as *Where Is Thumbkin?*)

> Where is our tree?
> Where is our tree? *(As you sing, pretend to search for the tree.)*
> Here it is.
> Here it is. *(As you sing, point to the tree.)*
> How are you today, tree?
> Very well, we thank you!
> Run around.
> Run around. *(As you sing, run around the tree.)*

Ask the children for ideas on how to care for the tree. Ideas could include watering it, hugging it, not pulling its leaves or bark, or giving it a present, such as flower at its base. If possible, try to act on one or more of the children's ideas.

End the game by having the children run around the tree. (Or run around all the trees if there are a bunch of them.) Then shout out, "Who loves trees?" And have the children shout back, "We do!"

18

Breaths of Love

Scripture: Love one another. (John 15:12-13)
This Game Teaches: To love others.
Materials: None

Game: Have the children sit in a circle. Read aloud John 15:12-13.

Say, "Loving each other is so important. We're going to play a game about love. Before we start, let's practice breathing in *(pause and demonstrate)* and breathing out *(pause and demonstrate)*."

Have the children practice breathing in and breathing out. Choose a category, such as one of these:

- Animals
- Family members
- Friends

Demonstrate how to breathe in and say "I love" and then breathe out and say someone or something from a specific category. For example, if you're starting with the category of animals, you might say "I love" while breathing in and "my cat, Rocky" as you breathe out.

Go around the circle and have each child do the activity. When everyone has done this once, choose a different category and play again.

End the game by having all the children breathe in together and say "I love" and then breathe out while saying "God."

Bonus Idea

Preschoolers like to test their limits, so play the game and have the person name as many things as possible with the exhalation. For example, if your category is family members, someone might say, "I love" while inhaling, and "Mom, Dad, Joey, Lisa, Grandpa, and Grandma" while exhaling. See how many people each child can name before running out of air.

19

Light of the World

Scripture: You are the light of the world. (Matthew 5:14-16)
This Game Teaches: We are to shine and use the talents God gave us.
Materials: A candle in a candle stand, a working flashlight

Game: Place a candle in a candle stand. Set it in the middle of the room. (Do not light the candle because of a fire hazard.)

Have the children form a circle around the candle. Read aloud Matthew 5:14-16. Then have children hold hands and sing this song to the tune of *Ring Around the Rosy* while they do the actions to the words:

> Ring around the candle. Let's see what we handle.
> Wobble. Wobble. We all fall down.

Replace the candle with the flashlight. (If you wish, you can turn the lights off in the room and turn on the flashlight so that the light is shining straight up.) Sing the song again to the same tune:

> Ring around the flashlight. Keep it shining
>   so bright
> Wobble. Wobble. We all fall down.

End the game by having the children sit in a circle in the dark. Pass around the lit flashlight. Have each child say, "I am the light of the world" while holding the lit flashlight before passing it to the child next to him or her.

Bonus Idea

Since preschoolers love stuffed animals, adapt this game with a stuffed cat. Sing this to the tune of Ring Around the Rosy while they do the actions to the words:

> Ring around the kitty. Who is cute and pretty?
> Meow. Meow. We all fall down.

Go God's Way

Scripture: Live good lives. Live God's way. (Ephesians 5:1-17)
This Game Teaches: We can choose to live in good ways.
Materials: None

Game: Have the children stand in a circle. Say, "Sometimes we get the grumpies. What makes you grumpy?" Let the children respond.

21

Say, "Oh! Oh! I feel the grumpy bug." Wiggle your leg and different parts of your body as if the grumpy bug is running around your body. You can pretend to pull the grumpy bug out of your pocket or out of your ear (or out of your nose). Then pretend to lose it and say that the grumpy bug has jumped onto another child. Keep talking about the grumpy bug as the children move and giggle.

At one point say, "I caught the grumpy bug!" Hold it between your two hands. Ask, "Who wants to throw the grumpy bug in the trash?" Give the pretend grumpy bug to another child to throw away. Don't be surprised if the child steps on it or wants to flush it down the toilet. The main point is that the child should throw away the grumpy bug.

Then say, "Oh! I feel the happy bug." Smile. "The happy bug makes me feel so good inside." Hug yourself. Pretend to pet the happy bug. "God wants us to live happy, helpful lives, not grumpy lives. I like it when I'm happy. I become happy when I help other people and when I'm nice to people."

Play the game again with the happy bug.

End the game by saying, "Oh look! There are a whole bunch of happy bugs! Let's each catch one and bring it home."

Bonus Idea

Teach children about other feelings by making them into imaginary bugs. For example, invent the angry bug (if you have children who hit when they get mad) or the talkative bug (if you have children who always interrupt).

Follow the Fun

Scripture: Your heart will be where your riches are. Give to the poor. (1 Chronicles 28: 8-10)
This Game Teaches: Follow God.
Materials: None

22

Game: Have the children sit in a circle. Say, "In the Bible, David said it was good to follow God. We're going to play a game about following David."

Stand in the middle of the circle. Say, "We're going to take turns being David. First, I'll be David. Let's start by having everyone say together, 'David, David, what should we do?'" Have the children ask the question. Then do a silly action such as using your hands to wiggle your ears while you say, "David says to wiggle your ears."

Then choose another child to be David. As a group, ask the child in the middle, "David, David, what should we do?" The child in the middle then chooses a silly action and says, "David says to _____ (name the action)." Then have the child in the middle choose another child to be David.

Keep playing the game until every child has been David at least once.

End the game by standing in the middle one last time. When the children ask what to do, say, "David says we should thank God." Then lead a thank-you prayer to God.

One Body, Many Parts

Scripture: Every part of the body is important, just like everybody is important. (1 Corinthians 12:12-31)
This Game Teaches: Every part is important.
Materials: None

Game: Have children spread out. Say, "The Bible says that every part of our body is important. We need our eyes, ears, feet, hands, heart—every single part. Let's play a game about our bodies."

Name body parts one at a time and have children try to do motions for that body part:

- What if you only had ears? How would your ears sniff the air? *(Sniff the air with your ear.)*
- What if you had only feet? How would you clap your feet? *(Sit on the floor and clap your feet.)*
- What if you had only eyes? How would you hear with your eyes? *(Try to hear with your eyes.)*
- What if you had only legs and no knees? How would you move? *(Walk stiffly around the room without bending your knees.)*

- What if you didn't have a neck? How would you move? *(Draw your shoulders up to hide your neck and try to walk around.)*
- What if you didn't have hands? How would you hold hands? *(Put your elbows next to someone else's elbows to hold elbows.)*
- What if you had only arms and no elbows? How would you move your arms? *(Keep your arms straight and pick up something without bending your elbows.)*
- What if you only had a mouth but no teeth? How would you talk? *(Pull in your lips and talk as if you didn't have teeth.)*

End the game by reading aloud 1 Corinthians 12:27. Say, "Let's thank God for our feet *(stomp feet)*, our hands *(clap hands)*, our mouths *(say alleluia)*, and every part of our body *(say hooray)*."

Who Hid the Boy?

Scripture: Joash's aunt hides Joash for seven years so that he is not killed. (2 Kings 11:1-3)
This Game Teaches: Protect each other from harm.
Materials: A small toy boy or small toy baby

Game: Say, "In the Bible, there were a bunch of bad guys who wanted to hurt children. One aunt hid her nephew for seven years to keep him safe. We're going to play a game where we hide this toy and try to keep it hidden from the person who is 'It'."

Have the children sit in a circle with their hands clasped behind their backs. Ask for two volunteers. Give one the small toy. Have the other volunteer stand in the middle of the circle and close his or her eyes.

Have the child holding the toy walk around the outside of the circle while the other children chant, "Safety. Safety. Let's hide the boy." At some point, the child gives the toy to one of the children. Then the child takes a seat in another part of the circle.

Have the child in the middle uncover his or her eyes. Give the child three guesses. If the person is correct in one of the guesses, the child holding the toy must go to the middle and the child that guessed correctly gets to walk around the circle and give the toy to someone else.

If the child in the middle does not guess correctly within three guesses, the child stays in the middle for one more game. The child holding the toy gets to identify him- or herself and be the one who walks around the outside of the circle and place the toy in a child's hand.

Play the game a number of times. End the game by having the children place their hands in front of them. Then pass the toy around the circle in front of the children while saying, "We all can help each other when we need help. Joash's aunt helped him, and we can help each other."

24

Who Can? I Can!

Scripture: Everything God created is good. (1 Timothy 4:4-5)
This Game Teaches: God made us and all the amazing things that
we do.
Materials: None

25

Game: Have the children spread out throughout the room.
Have them sit. Say, "Everything God created is good. God
created you and you and you." Point to each person. "We
have an amazing God."

Say, "What's more amazing is that we're growing and
learning to do more and more things. When I name something
that you can do, I want you to jump up and shout, 'I can.' Then sit
back down again and listen for the next thing I have to say."

Name things such as these (one at a time):
- Who can ride a tricycle?
- Who can ride a bike with training wheels?
- Who can brush his or her teeth without any help?
- Who can button his or her shirts?
- Who can zip a zipper?
- Who can say a word in English?
- Who can say a word in another language? (*Let the children who
jump up say what they know.*)
- Who can run really fast? (*Ask the children to run around the room
before they sit down again.*)
- Who can cross their fingers?
- Who can hop on one foot? (*Ask the children to hop around the
room before they sit down again.*)
- Who can whistle?
- Who can clap?
- Who can laugh? (*Ask everyone to laugh together.*)

End the game by having the children form a circle and hold
hands. Ask, "Who can raise their hands?" Have everyone raise their

hands in the air while holding hands. Ask, "Who can lower their hands?" Have everyone lower their hands while holding hands. Ask, "Who can clap for God for making all these great things we can do?" Together, clap.

Great Games for GRADES K-3

Playing games with children between the ages of five and nine usually is great fun. They are old enough to follow directions, but still young enough not to have started to develop an attitude.

A big component of playing games successfully with this age group is to create community. Help children learn each other's names. Whenever a game requires that they be with a small group or with a partner, encourage children to team up with different children each time. Playing is often how children at this age get to know each other.

Whenever you can, try to figure out ways to emphasize reading skills. Recognizing letters of the alphabet and reading simple words can excite the younger children in this age group. Second and third graders are often proud when they're asked to read aloud a passage of scripture.

Children at this age also are learning new physical skills. They're becoming more adept at throwing, catching, skipping, galloping, and hopping. Playing games such as the twenty-five games that follow help build and master their skills while also teaching children more about the Bible and faith.

Stomp Out Sin

Scripture: Turn from sin and turn toward God. (Romans 6:1-14)
This Game Teaches: We can resist temptation and not sin.
Materials: One box of paper cups (about 100) for bathroom
dispensers (or use Styrofoam® cups)

26

Game: Before the game, place paper cups upside down
throughout a play area. Keep children out of the area until you
play the game.

Say, "The Bible says not to sin. Sins are bad things that we
can do. What are some bad things that are easy to do?"

Encourage the children to give lots of examples.

Say, "We're going to play a game about stomping out sin. We'll
gather in the play area where we have all these cups set up. When I
tell you to start, begin stomping on the cups and flattening them."

Play the game.

End the game by
having children pick
up all the smashed
cups. Then take turns
throwing them in the
garbage and saying,
"throw out sin" as you
toss out the cups.

Weighed Down

Scripture: Evil thoughts and actions such as greed, pride, and jealousy make us unworthy. (Mark 7:20-23)
This Game Teaches: Evil thoughts and actions can weigh us down.
Materials: A foam ball, masking tape, three quarters

Game: Before you play, tape one quarter to a foam ball with masking tape. Have the children form a circle.

Explain that you're going to play catch. Give one child the ball and have him or her throw it to someone across the circle. Most likely, the ball will not go where the child intended it to go. Keep playing for a short while.

Say, "The Bible talks about evil thoughts and actions that can weigh us down. This ball is weighed down by jealousy. That's why it doesn't move well." Play a bit more. After about thirty seconds, ask for the ball. Tape two more quarters to the ball on different sides. Play again. The ball will become even more unstable. Say, "This ball is getting weighed down not only by jealousy but also greed and pride. No wonder it doesn't move well."

Ask for a volunteer to remove all three quarters. Play again. Ask children what a difference it makes for the ball not to be weighed down.

End the game by having the children list evil thoughts and actions. Talk about how they can choose to be good instead of bad.

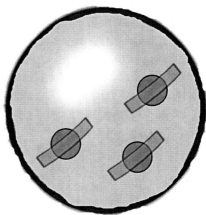

Grab the Manna

Scripture: People gather manna from the ground. (Exodus 16)
This Game Teaches: God always provides.
Materials: Two large bags of cotton balls, two buckets

Game: Before the game, place a line of cotton balls about six inches apart. Create two lines of cotton balls, one for each team.

28

Tell the story about people gathering manna from the ground in Exodus 16. Say that you're going to play a game about manna.

Form two teams of an equal number of players. If you have an odd number of children, have one team choose one child who will go twice.

Have the children form two lines. Give the first person in each line a bucket. Explain that when you say, "Go," the child with the bucket will run up to where the line of cotton balls starts, grab the first cotton ball, place it in the bucket, run back to the line, and hand the bucket to the next player in line. That person will then do the same thing: run up to the next cotton ball in line, scoop it up, place it in the bucket, and run back to the line to hand off the bucket to the next player.

Play the game. See which team can gather all their cotton balls first.

End the game by having the children throw the cotton balls into the air and then scurry to pick them all up again. Say, "God provided food called manna in the Old Testament. It appeared on the ground, and people scooped it up. God always provides for us."

Bonus Idea

Instead of creating a line of cotton balls, create two areas where the cotton balls are thrown all over the place. (Make them distinct areas so that the children know which cotton balls belong to each team.) Then have players take turns running to any one of the cotton balls and placing it in the bucket before returning to the team.

Careful Carry

Scripture: Paul sends his greetings, saying how hard everyone has worked. (Romans 16)
This Game Teaches: Greet each other and work hard.
Materials: A paper cup for each child, water, two chairs

29

Game: Say, "Paul wrote a letter to the Romans. In that letter, he mentioned individuals who worked hard and how we should greet and support them. We're going play a game about greeting and working hard."

Form two teams of an equal number of players. If you have an odd number of children, have one team choose one child who will go twice.

Have the children form two lines. Give each child a paper cup. Fill the cup of the first person in each line halfway with water.

Set up a chair about ten feet away from each team. Say, "When I tell you to start, the first person needs to walk carefully with the cup of water to the chair, around it, and back. When the first person reaches the second person in line, he or she needs to pour the water into the second person's cup while saying the second person's name. You want to pour carefully because you want to keep as much water as possible in the cup so that by the end, you still have a lot of water."

Play the game. Expect some spills.

End the game by having the children see how much water was left in the last cup. Say, "It's good to work hard. You did a great job of keeping a lot of water in your

cup and pouring it. I also like how you called each other by name. Each one of us is important, and we have a lot to share."

Bonus Idea

On a warm or hot day, play the game outside. Ask parents for permission to get their children wet. Start out with a full cup of water and see what happens.

Follow the King

Scripture: King Jehoshaphat saves his people from the bad guys (2 Chronicles 20)
This Game Teaches: Follow the advice of leaders who listen to God.
Materials: None

30

Game: Say: "In the Bible, there were a bunch of people who followed God, who were being attacked by bad guys. They had a king—King Jehoshaphat—who listened to God to save God's people."

Tell the children that you're going to be King Jehoshaphat. They are to jump and run around the room but keep an eye on you. Say, "I have kingly powers that can tell when the bad guys are coming. When the bad guys come, I won't be able to speak. I will sit down and cover my mouth. When you see me do this, follow me. Sit down. Cover your mouth. Don't make a sound."

Begin the game. Run with the children. After about a minute, sit down and cover your mouth. Watch how long it takes for all the children to follow your lead. Once everyone is sitting and quiet, jump up and say, "We're safe! Let's run and jump again." After about a minute, sit down and cover your mouth. Watch what happens.

Repeat this game one or two more times.

End the game by saying, "You were quiet and still when the bad guys were around. I am very proud of you. It's good to follow kings and leaders who listen closely to God."

Run, Run, Run

Scripture: Run toward the goal that God calls us to. (Philippians 3:12-14)
This Game Teaches: Participate in the game of life.
Materials: None

Game: Read aloud Philippians 3:12-14. Talk about how living the Christian life can sometimes be like being in a race. It's important to participate, and it's important to know what your goals are.

Explain that you're going to play a game where you run in different ways. Have the kids spread out around the room and name different ways to run (one by one):

- Run like you're very old
- Run like you're carrying a bucket of water on your head
- Run like you're a baby
- Run like you want to win the race
- Run like a bear is chasing you
- Run like you have one bad leg

End the game by having the children run as fast as they can from one area of the room to the other. Say, "God asks us to run the race set before us. Let's live the best lives we can."

Living God's Way

Scripture: There are many ways to live the Christian life well. (1 Thessalonians 5:12-28)

This Game Teaches: We can live as Christians by making good choices.

Materials: A beanbag (or make your own by placing dried beans into a sock and tying the end of the sock so that beans stay secure in the sock)

32

Game: Read aloud 1 Thessalonians 5:12-28. Have the children sit in a circle. Give one a beanbag.

Say, "We're going to play a game about living God's way. When you're ready to toss the beanbag to someone in the circle, name one way that God wants us to act. For example, you could say 'love one another' or 'be kind.' Ready? Let's play."

Encourage children to toss the beanbag gently. Don't be surprised if the first two children use the examples that you gave. Continue playing the game.

End the game by asking the children who should live God's way. Have the children toss the beanbag around the circle (in order of the circle) as they each say their name. End it with a big "Amen."

A Wicked Wind

Scripture: The wind blows things away, but God's love lasts forever. (Psalm 103:15-22)

This Game Teaches: God's love goes on and on—even when the wind blows.

Materials: A straw and ping-pong ball for each child, masking tape, a piece of yarn or string that you tape to the floor as the finish line

Game: Before the game, place a piece of yarn or string on the floor to mark the finish line. Secure each end of the yarn by taping it to the floor with masking tape.

Read aloud Psalm 103:15-22. Talk about how powerful the wind is. Ask the children about windstorms they have experienced.

Have the children line up across the room from the yarn finish line. Have the children kneel. Give each child a straw and a ping-pong ball. Ask for one child to demonstrate how you blow a ping-pong ball across the floor by blowing through the straw. Explain that the child cannot touch the ball with the straw. If he or she does, the child must go back to the beginning and start again.

Once the demonstration is done, have the children line up on their hands and knees. When you say, "Go," have them blow their ping-pong balls across the room until they get over the finish line.

End the game by saying, "Even though the wind blows and changes everything, the one thing that never changes is God's love."

The Lost Coin

Scripture: A woman loses a coin and searches for it until she finds it. (Luke 15:8-10)
This Game Teaches: It's worth investing time to find something that is lost.
Materials: One quarter

34

Game: Read aloud Luke 15:8-10. Then ask for a volunteer. Have the volunteer leave the room.

Ask one of the children to hide a quarter somewhere in the room. Make sure it's not hidden too well—or not hidden well enough. Check that everyone knows where the quarter is. Have the children spread out throughout the room.

Invite the volunteer back in. Explain that there is a lost coin. The volunteer can begin to move around the room, but the children cannot leave their stations. As the volunteer gets near a person, the person can say, "close" if the volunteer is getting close to the coin or "far" if the volunteer is getting far away from the coin.

Play the game until the volunteer finds the coin. Then ask for another volunteer and play the game again.

End the game by having one of the children place the quarter into the offering plate. Say, "It's good to look for things that are lost, and it's good to be generous with God."

Jumping in the Desert

Scripture: God's people wandered in the desert for forty years. (Deuteronomy 2:1-25)

This Game Teaches: When we do things over and over, we can become better and better.

Materials: A long strip of bubble wrap (the big-bubble kind), a clothespin for each child, markers

35

Game: Before you play the game, have each child write his or her name in large letters on a clothespin and then decorate it with markers.

Briefly tell the story about God's people wandering in the desert for forty years.

Lay a long strip of bubble wrap on the floor. Have children each hold their clothespins and line up behind the bubble wrap. As the adult, stand along the side of the bubble wrap and pinpoint where a child lands after jumping.

Have the first child jump. (Get ready for sound effects from the bubble wrap and the kids.) Mark where the child landed. Have the child attach his or her clothespin to the bubble wrap along the side to designate where he or she landed. Then have the child who jumped take your place to watch where the next child lands.

Have each child jump and mark his or her positions.

Then say, "God's people wandered in the desert for forty years. They did things over and over, and they got better and better. Let's see how we do with our second jumps. Try to jump farther this time than you did the first time."

Have the children jump again. If they jumped farther, move their clothespin to mark their new place. Otherwise leave their clothespin where it was originally.

End the game by having the children all jump and march on the bubble wrap at the same time. Say, "God's people stuck together during those forty years in the desert. When we stick together, we become stronger."

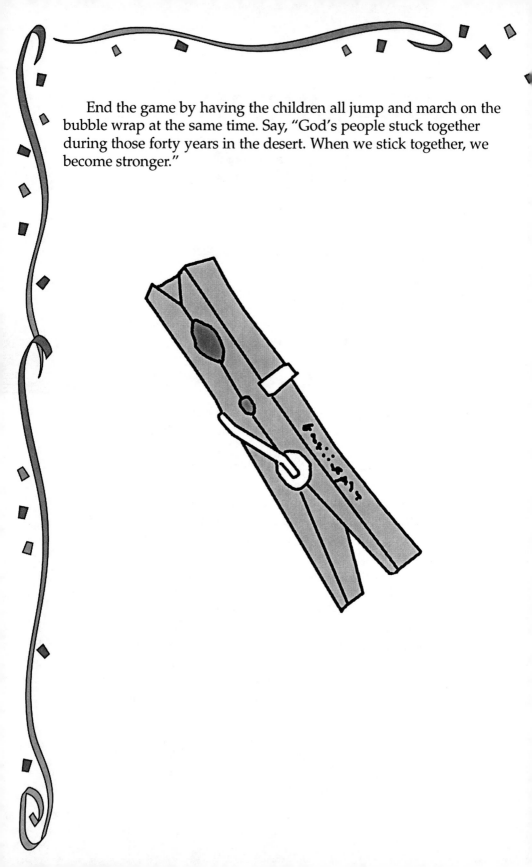

Shoe Confusion

Scripture: The Philistine army became confused, and everything turned to chaos. (1 Samuel 14:16-23)
This Game Teaches: God is with us during times of confusion.
Materials: None

Game: Have everyone (including the adults) take off his or her shoes. Make a huge pile of shoes at one end of the room. Have the kids stir the shoes so they become even more mixed up. Then have the children make the shoes into a large pile.

Say, "In 1 Samuel 14, the people became very confused. It's kind of like our shoe pile here. All the shoes are mixed up. Let's play a game about shoe confusion."

Have everyone (including the adults) line up at the other end of the room away from the shoe pile. When you say, "Go," have everyone run to the pile of shoes, dig through it, find their shoes, put their shoes on, tie their shoes, and run back to the beginning.

End the game by saying, "Even when life becomes confusing, God is always with us. The confusion story in 1 Samuel 14 ends with God saving the day. God still saves the day. Each one of us is now less confused because we have our shoes."

Jingle Praise

Scripture: A song of praise. (Psalm 33)
This Game Teaches: Praise God.
Materials: Four to six pipe cleaners per child, eight to twelve large jingle bells per child

37

Game: Before you play this game, make one arm bracelet and one ankle bracelet to show as an example. Slide two to three jingle bells onto a pipe cleaner and then tie it around your wrist or ankle. Ideally, you want the jingle bells to be spread out along the bracelet. Shake your arm (or your leg) to see how to make the bracelet jingle.

Say, "We're going to praise God. In Psalm 33, it says that it's good to praise God." If you wish, you can read a scripture passage, such as Psalm 33:1-3.

Before you praise God together, take time to make arm and ankle bracelets. (You might want to have another adult or some teenagers helping you.) Make sure each child makes at least one arm and one ankle bracelet. If you have enough supplies, have each child make two arm and two ankle bracelets so that they can wear four.

Once the bracelets are made and are on the children, praise God. Lead them in dance praises, such as these:

- Praise God by raising your arms in the air and shaking them.
- Praise God by jumping up and down.
- Praise God by making a circle, holding hands, and moving your arms up and down.
- Praise God by staying in the circle. Put your right foot in and shake it. Put your left foot in and shake it.
- Praise God by running around the room and shaking your arms.

End the game by having the children raise their arms into the air and shake them while saying, "Praise God."

A Cleaner Earth

Scripture: God created the earth. (Proverbs 3:19-21)
This Game Teaches: We should take good care of the earth.
Materials: A bunch of old newspapers, a laundry basket

Game: Before the game, open up newspaper sections. Cut or rip the newspaper section in half. Create a pile of this size paper.

Say, "God created the earth. Sometimes people make the earth a dirty place. They throw garbage all over."

Have the children take a piece of newsprint, wad it up into a ball and throw it somewhere on the floor in your playing area. Encourage them to make a number of these newspaper balls.

When the playing area is covered, have the children wash their hands. Place a laundry basket in the middle of the playing area.

Have the children spread out throughout the room. Make sure no child is closer than two feet to the laundry basket.

Say, "Let's clean up this mess. From where you are standing, try to throw the newspaper balls into the laundry basket. You can't move, so once you throw your balls, someone else may need to pick them up and try making a basket."

Play the game until the laundry basket is full and all the balls are off the floor.

End the game by having children wash their hands one more time. Say, "God likes it when we clean up the earth and clean up ourselves. God created a beautiful earth, and it's good to take good care of it."

Numbers That Count

Scripture: Animals two by two (Genesis 7), Jesus rose on the third day (Mark 16:1-11), forgive people seven times seventy (Matthew 18:21-22), twelve disciples (Luke 8:1-3), and Jesus was in the wilderness for forty days (Mark 1:12)

This Game Teaches: Certain numbers appear over and over in the Bible and kids can have fun while learning about these numbers.

Materials: Balloons

Game: Have the children stand in a playing area fairly close together. Inflate one balloon. Have the children practice batting the balloon and keeping it in the air.

Say, "In the Bible, certain numbers appear over and over. We're going to play a number game. I will give a number and brief description of that number from the Bible. See if you can keep the balloon in the air by batting it the number of times I told you. You can only bat the balloon two times in a row. Then someone else needs to bat it."

Play the game. Use these numbers:
- Two—Animals came two by two
- Three—Jesus rose on the third day
- Seven—Forgive people seven times seventy
- Twelve—There are twelve disciples
- Forty—Jesus was in the wilderness for forty days

End the game by making this joke: How about feeding the five thousand? Then see what's the highest number kids can get to by batting the balloon into the air.

Snakes Everywhere

Scripture: Snakes were biting and killing God's people. God told Moses to make a metal snake. When God's people were bitten, they could touch the metal snake and be healed. (Numbers 21:4-9)

This Game Teaches: When life gets difficult, God has solutions.

Materials: A large roll of crepe paper, scissors, marker, masking tape

Game: Before you play this game, cut a six-foot piece of crepe paper. Use the marker to draw two eyes at one end of the crepe paper to make a snake. Hang up the six-foot crepe paper snake with masking tape. Hang it low enough so that children can reach up and touch it when they're standing.

Cut a three-foot piece of crepe paper for each child. Have each child roll up their piece. Say, "In the Bible, snakes were biting God's people, and they were dying. We're going to play a snake game."

Have the children spread out throughout the room. Then have them throw their crepe paper so that it unravels. Say, "When I tell you to move, I want you to go from where you are standing to this side of the room *(point to one side of the room)*. You need to walk carefully. If you step on a piece of crepe paper, you need to fall down like it bit you, and you died."

Play the game. Then say, "People in the Bible didn't know what to do, so God told Moses how to help them. Moses made a big snake out of metal." Point to the snake that you have hung up. "We will play the game again. If you step on a crepe-paper snake this time, immediately go to the big healing snake. Touch it, and you can keep playing."

Play the game again.

End the game by having the children each pick up a crepe paper snake to take home with them. Say, "Even when life gets difficult, God is with us. When we get sick, God can heal us."

Watch Out for Saul

Scripture: Saul tried to hurt David. (1 Samuel 19)
This Game Teaches: God can protect you if you also protect yourself.
Materials: None

41

Game: Ask for a volunteer. The volunteer will be David.

Say, "In 1 Samuel 19, David was good friends with Jonathan. But Jonathan's dad wanted to hurt David. Jonathan's dad's name was Saul. Saul wanted to hurt David."

Explain that you're going to be playing a game like Duck, Duck, Goose. Have all the children sit in a circle except for the volunteer who will be David.

Have the volunteer walk around the circle tapping each child on the head while saying "friend." At one point, the volunteer should tap one child's head and say "Saul." Whoever is called Saul should jump up and chase David around the circle. If Saul catches David, the child has to sit in the middle. Then Saul becomes the new David.

Keep playing until you have a few Davids in the middle of the group.

End the game by saying, "Saul tried to hurt David, but Jonathan helped keep David safe. We can help each other, and God can help us too."

Crossing the Red Sea

Scripture: The Red Sea opened up so God's people could escape the Egyptians. (Exodus 14)
This Game Teaches: Sometimes you have to run fast to escape.
Materials: None

42

Game: Ask for a volunteer. Have the volunteer stand in the middle of a playing area with his or her back toward the other children. If you have more than ten children present, have two volunteers.

Have the children line up on one side of the room. Say, "In the book of Exodus, the Red Sea opened up for a brief time so that God's people could escape the bad guys. We're going to play a game about the Red Sea."

Explain that at some point you're going to say, "Open sea." As soon as you do, the children should start running from one side of the room to the other. When you say, "Closed sea," the volunteer can turn around and start chasing the kids to tag them. The kids can decide to continue across the playing area or return to the beginning line. They can be safe at either destination as long as they don't get tagged.

If any child gets tagged, he or she becomes the new volunteer to stand in the middle. Play the game again after you have all the children return to one side.

End the game by saying "Open sea" so that everyone makes it to the other side. Then say, "God opened the Red Sea so that all of God's people could escape. I am glad we have such a helpful God."

United Together

Scripture: We are united with each other and with Christ. (Philippians 2:1-5)
This Game Teaches: We are all connected.
Materials: A ball of yarn, a spoon

Game: Before you play the game, tie the end of the ball of yarn to the spoon so that it's secure.

43

Have the children form a circle. Say, "Philippians says that we are all connected to each other and with Christ. We're going to play a game that connects us together."

Give one child the ball of yarn tied to the spoon. Have the child hold the ball of yarn with one hand while he or she uses the other hand to drop the spoon down his or her shirt. (You may need to help the child so that the ball of yarn unwinds as the spoon moves.)

Have the child hand the spoon to the child next to him or her. (Choose a direction to go: either clockwise or counterclockwise.) Have the second child take the spoon and move it up inside his or her shirt so that the spoon comes out the top.

Then have the second child hand it to the third child who drops the spoon down his or her shirt. Note: With each child, the spoon will travel either up or down the shirt. Each child should do the opposite of the child next to him or her. You may also want to give the first child some assistance to make sure the ball of yarn continues to unroll easily.

Continue until the spoon has traveled all the way around the circle and all the children are connected.

End the game by saying, "We are all connected. What one person does affects another person. Let's be kind to one another."

Bonus Idea

If you have a cross or other Christian symbol, consider including that in your circle. (The spoon can wrap around it.) This can show the kids how they are connected to Christ and to each other.

Melt Away

Scripture: Whatever manna the people did not eat, the sun melted it away. (Exodus 16:15-21)
This Game Teaches: God provides for us every day.
Materials: An ice cube for every three children

44

Game: Create groups of three (or four) children. Say, "In the Bible, God gave the people food every day. Whatever food that was left over, melted away. We're going to play a game about melting." Give each group an ice cube.

Explain that children can rub the ice cube, place it in the sun, or blow on it, but they cannot try to break the ice cube into small pieces or scrape it. Give groups a few minutes to see what happens.

End the game by having the groups line up their ice cubes side by side. See which one melted the most. Find out which techniques the group used to help the cube melt faster. Then say, "We can do some things to help the ice melt, but God does most of the work. We need to do our part, but we also need to trust God to do God's part."

Lame Legs Become Strong Legs

Scripture: A lame man is healed. (Acts 3:1-10)
This Game Teaches: Miracles can happen.
Materials: Balloons, a way to designate a turnaround area for a race, such as going around a chair or crossing a line

Game: Form two teams of an equal number of players. If you have an odd number of children, have one team choose one child who will go twice.

Have the children form two lines. Give the first child in each line an inflated balloon. Say, "In the Bible, there were lame people. That meant that they could not walk. In the book of Acts, Peter healed a lame man. We're going to play a game about the lame man."

Explain that when you start the game, the first person in each line should move the balloon across the floor to the designated point (such as around a chair or crossing a line). However, the child must move on his or her hands and knees and try to move the balloon with his or her head or hands. Once the child has reached the designated point, the child is healed and can walk

and run. The child can then jump up onto his or her feet, pick up the balloon, run back to the line, and pass off the balloon to the next child in line.

The next child, however, is lame and must move the balloon to the designated point on his or her hands and knees. Once he or she is healed at the designated point, then the child can run back with the balloon to hand it off to the third person in line.

End the game by having the children in each line pass the balloon from child to child saying, "It's a miracle; it's a miracle. God healed lame people so they could walk."

Feeling Faces for Different Times

Scripture: There is a time for everything. (Ecclesiastes 3:1-12)
This Game Teaches: There are times when we'll be happy and times when we'll be sad.
Materials: A Bible

46

Game: Have the children spread out through a play area. Say, "There is a famous part of the Bible where it talks about good things happening and bad things happening. I'm going to read aloud this scripture from Ecclesiastes, and I want you to make a face or body stance for each action that I read."

Slowly read aloud Ecclesiastes 3:1-12. Pause after every major change. For example, in verse two, pause after birth (and see what faces the children make) and then pause after death (and see what faces the children make). Continue in this way until you have read through verse 12.

End the game by having the children form a circle and hold hands. Have the children raise their hands while you say, "God

gives us times when we are happy and up." Then have children lower their hands and heads while you say, "And God gives us times when we are sad and down." Then have everyone raise his or her heads and hands while you say, "But no matter what happens, God is always with us."

I Spy

Scripture: When two or three gather in God's name, God is with them. (Matthew 18:19-20)
This Game Teaches: Elements of worship.
Materials: An empty sanctuary

47

Game: Gather in an empty sanctuary. Make sure a worship bulletin is nearby. Read aloud Matthew 18:19-20 from the Bible.

Say, "When we worship God, we use a lot of different things. Let's see how many things you can spy from a worship service."

Name these things one by one and have the children walk over to these items to identify where they are (and take a closer look):

- I spy a Bible.
- I spy a cross.
- I spy empty offering envelopes.
- I spy a pulpit.
- I spy the rope for the church bell (if your church has one, and it may be outside the sanctuary).
- I spy the baptismal font.
- I spy a worship bulletin.
- I spy a pew (or chairs).
- I spy an organ (or a piano or guitars).
- I spy a hymnal (or music book).
- I spy the balcony.
- I spy the altar.
- I spy the stained-glass windows.

- I spy the worship attendance sheets.
- I spy the communion rail.
- I spy the offering plate.

  End the game by asking children to name something they spy. (Children often notice things that adults often don't.)

Bonus Idea

Expand the I Spy game to your entire church. Have children spy where the church office is, the library, the bathrooms, the nursery, the chapel, the pastor's office, the kitchen, the fellowship hall, the choir room, Sunday school rooms, the church van, and other significant rooms and items in your church.

One-by-One Thanks

Scripture: God gives us many gifts. (2 Corinthians 9:10-15)
This Game Teaches: Be thankful.
Materials: Balloons, yarn, scissors

48

Game: String a piece of yarn around one stable object on one side of
your room and extend the yarn across the room before
securing it to another stable object on the opposite side of your
room. (Ideally, you want the yarn dividing your play area in
half so that children can comfortably stand on both sides of
the yarn and play this game.) Inflate
a couple of balloons.

Have the children form two lines, one
on each side of the yarn. You want
approximately the same number of
children on both sides. (It's okay if one
side has one more child than the other.)

Say, "Second Corinthians says we have
much to be thankful for. God gives us
many great things. We're going to play a
thankful game. I'm going to start a balloon
at this end of the line. I want you to tap the
balloon and name one thing you're thankful for in the category that
I've named. Tap the balloon over the yarn to the child in front of
you. Then the next child will tap the balloon while naming
something to be thankful for to the child across the yarn who is next
in line. Ideally, the balloon will move all the way down the line so
that everyone gets to tap it once and name one thing to be thankful
for. If the balloon falls, pick it up and keep going."

Have children name something they're thankful for in a specific
category. For example, if the category is colors, each child will name
a color down the line. (It's okay if children name the same colors
because they're naming what they're most thankful for.)

Categories include:
- Colors
- Mealtime foods
- Pets
- Snack foods
- Physical activities
- Toys
- TV shows
- People
- Places

Once the balloon reaches the end of the line, choose another category and start another balloon. Play the game three or four times, using three or four categories.

End the game by having the children play the game one more time. This time have them name what they're most thankful for.

The Joy of Laughter and Praise

Scripture: When you're happy, sing praises. (James 5:13-18)
This Game Teaches: Laugh and sing when you're happy.
Materials: Musical instruments, such as sticks, tambourines, maracas, and others

49

Game: Have the children each find a partner. If there's an extra child, make a group of three.

Read aloud James 5:13. Say, "We're going to play two happy games. The first game is a laughing game. In your groups, decide who will go first. Then that person will make funny, silly faces and try to make the other person laugh. See how long it takes."

Play the game. After a bit, have children switch so the other has a turn to make the other laugh.

Then give children each a musical instrument. Sing the song *When You're Happy and You Know It*. Instead of clapping hands, have children make music with their instruments during the clapping part. Sing:

When you're happy and you know it, make some noise.
When you're happy and you know it, make some noise.
When you're happy and you know it, then your face will
surely show it.
When you're happy and you know it, make some noise.

End the game by having the children march around the room playing their instruments.

Trinity Triangles

Scripture: The trinity: God, Christ, and the Holy Spirit. (2 Corinthians 13:11-13)
This Game Teaches: The trinity includes the Father, the Son, and the Holy Spirit.
Materials: Butcher paper or newsprint, scissors (If you use newsprint, open a newspaper section to the middle and use that size, which is 21 1/2 inches by 24 inches.)

50

Game: Before you play the game, cut butcher paper or newsprint into large triangles. Make enough triangles so that three children can stand on each one with one or two children left over. For example, if you usually have ten children present, cut three triangles. If you usually have twenty children, cut six triangles. Place the triangles on the floor in a playing area. Spread out the triangles.

Ask, "When we talk about the trinity, who is in the trinity?" Let the children answer.

Say, "We're going to play a game about the trinity." Ask for three children to volunteer. Have the three children stand on one triangle, each in one corner. Explain that the three volunteers will skip and sing around the room, and when you yell out "Trinity," they need to find a corner of one of the triangles to stand on to make up a trio with two other children. Note that either one or two children will be left over when all the children play.

Play the game with all the children. Have the children sing a favorite upbeat Christian song, such as *The B-I-B-L-E*, or *Praise Him, Praise Him*, or *I've Got the Joy, Joy, Joy, Joy Down in My Heart*.

Periodically yell out, "trinity," and watch the children scramble. Always make note of who gets left out. Play the game a number of times so that everyone gets turn.

End the game by having the children form a circle and hold hands. Say, "Let's go around the circle and say who's in the trinity, one by one." The first child says, "Father," the second says, "Son," the third says, "Holy Spirit." Then keep going around the circle until every child has named one part of the trinity. Be sure to end with "Holy Spirit."

Great Games for GRADES 4-6

Playing games with fourth- to sixth-graders involves stimulating their minds as well as their bodies. Many are doing complex work in school, and they are up for the challenge in Christian education as well.

Besides having fun, I enjoy engaging children in the upper elementary ages with tough questions. When we recently played the game "Good Neighbors," (which follows as game number 51), not only did naming countries around the world stimulate kids, but they got into an intense conversation when I started asking them questions, such as these:

- Does the story about the Good Samaritan mean that we help all of our neighbors? *(Yes, the kids said. Everyone is our neighbor.)*
- What about people who are disabled? *(Absolutely.)*
- What about people who have a different skin color? *(Yes. Skin color doesn't matter.)*

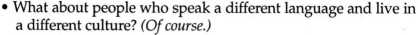

- What about people who speak a different language and live in a different culture? *(Of course.)*
- What about the bully at school? *(There was a pause. Then some of the kids said no.)*
- What about terrorists? *(Absolutely not. Not a single child in the class would stop for a terrorist.)*

I told them I was confused. If everyone was our neighbor, why didn't that include bullies and terrorists? The conversation became heated. Hadn't I seen what the terrorists had done to the Twin Towers? Didn't I think that was evil? Wasn't I afraid that a terrorist could hurt me?

I agreed. I believe terrorist acts are evil, but I also believed terrorists are our neighbors.

That made some upset. Then one finally said, "Okay, I'll help the terrorist only if I can disarm him so he doesn't hurt me. But then I'd turn him over to the police, and I would make sure we tortured him."

I asked the kids to open up their Bibles and re-read the story of the Good Samaritan. I asked where the Good Samaritan turned the hurt person over to the police and had the person tortured.

"That person was not a terrorist," one child said.

"How do you know?" I asked. I reminded them that in Bible times Jews thought Samaritans were terrorists and Samaritans thought Jews were terrorists.

We could have talked all day.

Even though I was unsettled by how much hatred these children had toward terrorists and bullies, I also understood their feelings. We live during unsettling times, but so did people who lived when the Bible was being written.

The next time I taught these children, we played more games. We got another stimulating discussion going.

Who said Christian education with children was dull?

Good Neighbors

Scripture: Parable of the Good Samaritan. (Luke 10:25-37)
This Game Teaches: Help all your neighbors.
Materials: A ball of yarn and a globe

Game: Have children gather around a globe. Ask, "Where do your neighbors live?" After children have responded, spin the globe, stop it, and stick your finger on a country. Ask, "Do your neighbors live here?" Spin the globe a few more times and repeat. Make the point that our neighbors are everywhere.

Have the children form a circle. Pull out a ball of yarn. Ask, "Who are your neighbors in here?" If a child doesn't make the point, talk about how everyone in your classroom is your neighbor—even if they don't live next door.

Say, "We're going to play a game about neighbors. First I will name a country where neighbors live. Then I'll call out one child's name. Then I'll throw the ball of yarn to that child while holding onto the loose end of the yarn. When you get the yarn, name another country (or state or city), hold onto a piece of the yarn, name another child across the circle and throw the ball of yarn while holding onto your piece of yarn." Point out that you're weaving a web, and everyone needs to hang on.

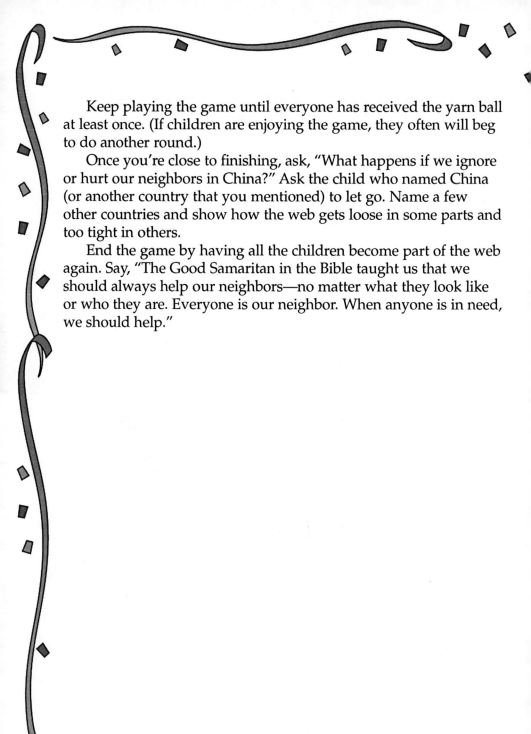

Keep playing the game until everyone has received the yarn ball at least once. (If children are enjoying the game, they often will beg to do another round.)

Once you're close to finishing, ask, "What happens if we ignore or hurt our neighbors in China?" Ask the child who named China (or another country that you mentioned) to let go. Name a few other countries and show how the web gets loose in some parts and too tight in others.

End the game by having all the children become part of the web again. Say, "The Good Samaritan in the Bible taught us that we should always help our neighbors—no matter what they look like or who they are. Everyone is our neighbor. When anyone is in need, we should help."

So Many Brothers!

Scripture: Joseph has eleven brothers who are jealous of him. (Genesis 35:22-26 and Genesis 37)

This Game Teaches: Jealousy can lead people to hurt others.

Materials: Thirteen pieces of colored construction paper (as many colors as you can find, and it's okay to have duplicate colors), marker, and small things for children to throw (such as acorns, small stones, or buttons)

Game: Before the game, write one of these names on each of the colored pieces of paper so that each paper has only one name:

- Jacob
- Joseph
- Reuben
- Simeon
- Levi
- Judah
- Issachar
- Zebulun
- Benjamin
- Dan
- Naphtali
- Gad
- Asher

Place the thirteen pieces of colored paper in one area of the room so that the children can surround the thirteen pieces of colored paper.

Have the children form a circle around the colored paper lying on the ground. Give each child a handful of small things (acorns, small stones, or buttons). Say, "In Genesis, Jacob had twelve sons, and his favorite son was Joseph. He gave Joseph an amazing colorful coat, and the eleven brothers were jealous. They tried to hurt Joseph. They stole his coat and placed blood on it. They told their dad that Joseph was dead. Instead, Joseph was alive and sold as a slave."

Explain that you're now going to begin the game. Say that you'll ask a question and the children will need to toss one small item onto the piece of paper that has the correct answer. Use questions such as these:

- Who was the father of the twelve brothers? *(Answer: Jacob)*
- Who received the amazing, colorful coat? *(Answer: Joseph)*
- Who was mean to Joseph? *(Answer: anyone but Jacob and Joseph)*
- Who said Joseph was dead? *(Answer: anyone but Jacob and Joseph)*
- Who was sad about Joseph being dead? *(Answer: Jacob)*
- Who was sold into slavery? *(Answer: Joseph)*

End the game by saying, "Jealousy can lead us to hurt people—even people in our own families. Joseph brothers were mean to Joseph, which made Joseph and Jacob sad. When we're jealous, let's talk about it before we start acting mean."

Bonus Idea

You can do more of the story by summarizing Genesis chapters 40–45. Or adapt this game to another scripture, especially a scripture that has a lot of details, such as Numbers 22 (with Balaam, the angel, and the talking donkey) or Acts 12 (where an angel visits Peter in jail).

Unfortunately, Fortunately

Scripture: Jesus is tempted by the Devil. (Matthew 4:1-11)
This Game Teaches: Although bad things happen, good things happen, too.
Materials: Bibles, paper, something to write with

53

Game: Form groups of three (or four). Ask the children to open their Bibles to Matthew 4:1-11. Have them read the scripture in their small groups. Then have them make two lists on a sheet of paper. Have them label one column "Unfortunately" and the other column "Fortunately."

Have groups write all the bad, unfortunate things that happen in Matthew 4 (in order) under the "Unfortunately" column. Then have them write all the good, fortunate things that happen in the scripture passage.

When the groups finish, have the children take turns reading aloud the unfortunate and fortunate things that happen. For example:

- Fortunately, the spirit led Jesus into the desert.
- Unfortunately, Jesus was tempted by the Devil in the desert.
- Unfortunately, Jesus was hungry after forty days and forty nights without food.
- Unfortunately, the Devil tempted Jesus to turn stones to bread so he could get something to eat.
- Fortunately, Jesus refused.

Continue until the kids have finished. Then ask: "How does the story start out: with a fortunate or unfortunate event? How does it end? What does this scripture tell us about temptation?"

End the game by praying aloud with the children, "Fortunately, we have had this time to study God's word together. Unfortunately, we must end this game. Fortunately, we can get together again soon. Amen."

Bonus Idea

Periodically use this format in studying other scripture passages. It helps kids dig into the scriptures more deeply.

Without Help; With Help

Scripture: Ruth says she will go with Naomi and help her. (Ruth 1)

This Game Teaches: We can do more when we help each other.

Materials: A laundry basket, five Frisbees®, two plastic bats, and a timer

Game: Have the children form a line about ten feet away from the laundry basket. Say that kids will take turns throwing the Frisbees® into the laundry basket. After the first one tries; the second one tries. If someone misses, wait until all five Frisbees® have been thrown before you run out to get them and try again.

Explain that you'll time how long it takes to throw the five Frisbees® into the laundry basket. Play the game. Once the five Frisbees® have made it into the laundry basket, tell the kids how long it took them.

Ask for two volunteers. Give each one a plastic bat. Have them stand near the laundry basket. Explain that you'll play the game again. This time, however, the children with the bats can try to stop the overthrown Frisbees® and bat them into the basket. (At first this will be tricky, but kids will catch on.) Say you'll time them again. Play the game.

At the end of the game, compare the two times. The second time will be faster than the first time. Tell the story about Naomi and Ruth. Say, "When we help each other, we can get more done, and then we can have more fun."

Sick and then Cured

Scripture: Naaman was sick with leprosy and then he was cured. (2 Kings 5)
This Game Teaches: The power of healing
Materials: None

55

Game: Count the number of children you have. For every six children, ask for a volunteer to be a germ and another volunteer to be a healer. (For example, if you had twelve children, you would have two germs and two healers.)

Explain that this is a game of double tag. You want to avoid being tagged by a germ. If you are, you must fall to the ground because you're sick and yell for a healer. If a healer tags you when you're on the ground, you are healed and can get up and play.

Caution the kids, however, that germs can get healers sick. If a healer is tagged by a germ, he or she must fall to the ground and wait for another healer to tag him or her. If all the healers are tagged, then the game is over.

Play the game. Consider playing it again with different children being the germs and the healers.

End the game. Say, "Like today, people who got sick in the Bible wanted to be healed. In 2 Kings 5, Elisha had the healing touch. In the New Testament, Jesus healed people. Let's thank God for people who work hard to heal others."

Scripture Scramble

Scripture: Abraham and Sarah (Genesis 17-18), Isaac (Genesis 22), Jacob, Leah, and Rachel (Genesis 29), Deborah (Genesis 35), Joseph (Genesis 37), Moses (Exodus 3), Joshua (Joshua), John the Baptist (Matthew 3), Judas Iscariot (Matthew 26), Peter (Mark 14:29-31), Elizabeth (Luke 1), Martha and Mary (Luke 10:38-42), Lazarus (John 11), Thomas (John 14:5), Paul (Acts 9), and Lydia (Acts 16:12-15)

This Game Teaches: Important people appeared in the Old and New Testaments.

Materials: Four buckets, twenty ping-pong balls, permanent marker, two paper lunch bags, four index cards, masking tape

Game: Before the game, use the permanent marker to write one name on each of the ping-pong balls. The twenty names (for the twenty ping-pong balls) include: Abraham, Moses, Isaac, Jacob, Joseph, Leah, Rachel, Sarah, Joshua, Deborah, Paul, John the Baptist, Judas Iscariot, Peter, Martha, Mary, Thomas, Elizabeth, Lazarus, and Lydia.

Place five balls with names from the Old Testament into each of the paper lunch bags. One bag will have Abraham, Isaac, Joseph, Rachel, and Deborah. The other will have Moses, Jacob, Leah, Sarah, and Joshua.

Place five additional balls into each paper lunch bag with names from the New Testament. One bag will have Paul, Judas Iscariot, Martha, Elizabeth, and Lazarus. The other will

have John the Baptist, Peter, Mary, Thomas, and Lydia. The paper bags should now have ten ping-pong balls with five from the Old Testament and five from the New Testament. Fold over the top of the bag so that you cannot see what's inside it.

Then write Old Testament on two of the index cards and New Testament on the other two index cards. With masking tape, secure an index card to each of the four buckets. Place two buckets about twenty feet in front of each team, one labeled as Old Testament and the other as New Testament.

Form two teams of an equal number of players. It's okay if you have an odd number of children; each team will get ten chances.

Have the children form two lines. Give the first person in line one of the folded-over bags. Say, "We're going to have a race to see how well you know people in the Bible. When I tell you to go, open the bag and pull out one ball. It will have the name of a person on it. Give the bag to the person standing behind you. Run to the buckets and place the ball in either the Old Testament or New Testament bucket, depending on where this person appears in the Bible. For example, if you pulled out the name Matthew, you would run and place it in the New Testament bucket because Matthew is a disciple in the New Testament. If you're not sure where the person appears, guess. Run back and tag the next person. Then that person can open the bag and pull out a ball. Go for speed and accuracy."

Play the game. Make note of which team finished first. Then have teams gather around one team's set of buckets. Check to see how many were correct. Then do the other team's.

End the game by having the children place all the balls into one bucket. Have the group count the balls. Read aloud Luke 12:33-34 and say how it's better to give than to receive.

Bonus Idea

After the game, have kids research each person in the Bible (using the scriptures above) to learn more about each person.

Give a Big Hand for God's Love

Scripture: God's love for us is great. (Ephesians 2:4-10)
This Game Teaches: We can use our hands to show God's love.
Materials: Washable dark markers

Game: Form two teams of about an equal number of players. Have the teams form a line, face the other team, and stand about three feet apart.

Have the children hold the palms of their hands out toward you. If you have a small number of kids (such as about five in each line), write one letter of the alphabet (large) on each of their two hands. If you have a large number of kids (such as about nine in each line), write one letter of the alphabet on only one of their hands. (Write the letter so that the top of the letter is at the top of their palm and the bottom of the letter is at the bottom of their palm.)

Write these letters (one on each palm of one team): D, E, G, I, L, O, O, S, V. Then write the same letters on the palms of the second teams.

Say, "God loves us very much. The Bible tells this to us over and over, and it says it again in Ephesians 2. When I tell you to go, I want you to use your hands to spell words and phrases that I name. Let's see which team can do each one first. You may need to cross one of your hands over someone else's. When you're finished, the other team should be able to see what you have spelled."

Spell words and phrases such as these (one at a time):
- Go love
- God lives

- Do give
- Good lives
- God loves
- I love God

When you're finished, ask teams to figure out other words and phrases they can spell. Some examples they may do include: dig, loose, dove, log, slid, igloo, goose, dive, and sold.

If you have only a small number of kids (such as two to six), consider using the letters: A, C, E, I, R, S. Spell words and phrases such as: cares, scare, race, I care, cars, scar, case, race, acre, rise, air, rice, ace, and ice.

End the game by having the kids spell God Loves with their hands one more time.

Bonus Idea

Have the children take off their socks and shoes. Write letters on the bottoms of their feet instead.

All of Me

Scripture: God is love. God loves every part of us. (1 John 4:7-21)
This Game Teaches: Everything about us matters to God.
Materials: A bunch of blank index cards, pen

Game: Before you play this game, write one of the following words on an index card. (Each index card will have one word on it when you're done, and each index card will be different.) Write these words on the index cards: Adventuresome, Beautiful, Creative, Disappointed, Enthusiastic, Funny, Giggle, Happy, Inspired, Joyful, Kind, Lazy, Mad, Nervous, Optimistic, Pressured, Quiet, Restless, Scared, Tired, Unhappy, Vulnerable, Worried, Extra Excited, Yawn, and Zippy. Mix up the cards when you're done.

58

If you have more than ten children present, create groups of less than ten children. Divide the cards up between the groups.

Say, "God is love. Because God is love, God loves everything about us. God loves us when we're happy and when we're sad. God cares about what happens to us."

Have each group place the index cards in a pile face down. Have children in the group take turns choosing one card. Have the person who chose the card show the word to the rest of the group and tell about a time he or she felt the way described on the card.

End the game by having the children put all the cards together. Then have them work as a large group and place the cards in alphabetical order. Say, "God loves everything about us. God cares about what happens to us and the choices we make. God is always there for us."

Come Together

Scripture: Come together and worship God. (Isaiah 45:20-25)
This Game Teaches: We can create a community that follows God.
Materials: Two oranges

59

Game: Form two teams of an equal number of players. If you have an odd number of children, have one team choose one child who will go twice.

Have the children form two lines. Designate a place about ten feet away from the front of each line. Mark it with a chair or masking tape on the floor.

Ask for two volunteers to demonstrate. Have the volunteers face each other and hold an orange between their two foreheads. (They may find that hugging each other will help keep the orange in place.) Then have the volunteers walk across the room without dropping the orange.

Say that you will have a race. The first two children of each line will place an orange between them on their foreheads. They need to move toward the designated line and back. If they drop the orange, they must stop, place the orange into position and then continue. When they reach the front of the line, the next two children will take the orange and do the same thing.

Play the game. See who can finish the game first.

End the game by saying that we can create a community that follows God. As a community not only can we worship God but we also can have fun together.

What's Hidden, What's Seen

Scripture: Achan gets into trouble for hiding things. (Joshua 7:20-26)
This Game Teaches: Life becomes difficult when we try to hide things.
Materials: Ten diverse objects that fit in your hand, such as a button, a rubber band, a pencil, a cotton ball, a bandage, a spoon, a napkin, as straw, an apple, and a rock

Game: Have the children sit in a circle. Place the ten objects in front of one of the children. Say that in the Bible a person named Achan got into trouble for hiding things. Explain that you're going to play a game where you can see some objects while others are hidden.

Designate which way objects will move around the circle: clockwise or counterclockwise. Before you play, say, "The first time things travel around the circle, they will travel in front of everyone. The second time, you need to pass the objects behind your back. The third time the objects move to the front. The fourth time the objects move behind your back." (This becomes tricky if children don't concentrate.)

Play the game. Have the first child begin passing objects. As objects come around the circle, remind them to pass them behind their backs the second time around.

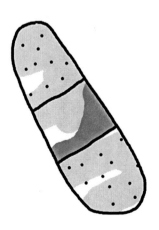

End the game by having the children place all the items into a pile. Talk about why we hide things and keep things secret. Say, "God doesn't want us to hide things from God. God wants us to do what's right."

Bonus Idea

To add a level of craziness to the game, consider including objects that aren't easy to pass, such as an ice cube, a wet bar of soap, or a handful of pennies.

Shave Samson's Head

Scripture: Delilah tricks Samson so he goes to sleep. She then gets a man to cut off his hair, which causes Samson to lose his strength. (Judges 16:18-22)

This Game Teaches: People can hurt you.

Materials: A paper cup and craft (or Popsicle®) stick for each child, shaving cream

Game: Ask each child to find a partner. If you have an extra child, create a group of three. Give each child a paper cup and a craft stick. Spray some shaving cream into each child's cup. Choose a play area that can get a bit messy. If it's warm, consider going outside.

Briefly tell the story of Samson and Delilah. Then have the children take the shaving cream and smear it around the cheeks and chin of their partner.

Say, "When I say go, use your craft stick to shave off the shaving cream from your partner's face. Think about Samson getting his hair shaved off."

Play the game. Afterward, have the children clean up.

End the game by asking someone to tell the story about Samson and Delilah.

Which Animal Am I?

Scripture: God created all kinds of animals—on the land, in the water, and in the air. (Genesis 1)

This Game Teaches: God created a wide variety of animals.

Materials: A pad of sticky notes (an ideal size is 3 inches by 3 inches)

Game: Before the game, write one animal name on each of the sticky notes so that each child will have one sticky note. The animals listed are in order of land, water, and air (so that if you have three or twenty-five children present you can have a variety):

- Gorilla
- Dog
- Cat
- Whale
- Goldfish
- Catfish
- Eagle
- Blue Jay
- Sparrow
- Cow
- Pig
- Elephant
- Shark
- Eel

- Salmon
- Seagull
- Stork
- Hawk
- Horse
- Lion
- Chipmunk
- Piranha
- Minnow
- Dolphin
- Cardinal
- Parrot
- Canary

To play the game, place a sticky note with an animal name on the forehead of each child. (Hide the sticky note so that the child having the one placed on his or her forehead cannot see it.) It's okay that everyone else can read what a person's animal is.

When you begin play, have children walk around the room. When you say, "Animal pairs," each child should find a partner. Let them ask one yes- or no-question, such as "Am I a land animal?" (If you have an extra child, have that child ask you a question.)

Once the questions are done, say, "Animal walk." Children then start walking around the room. Then say, "Animal pairs" when you want them to find another partner and ask another question.

As soon as one child figures out his or her animal, have that child shout out, "Animal Aware!" and tell the group his or her animal. Continue the game until everyone has figured out his or her animal. Note: You may need to give clues at the end if a child is having trouble figuring out his or her animal.

End the game by saying that we have a creative God who created many, many animals. Ask kids for their favorite animal and if they're worried about any animals. Then pray, thanking God for the animals.

Bonus Idea

If you're learning more about Noah's Ark (Genesis 7-8), create sticky notes where you make two of each animal. Once children figure out their animal, they then need to find their partner. The trick, however, is if their partner doesn't know which animal he or she has, the child cannot tell him or her. The child can only answer one question and try to stay close by until the child figures it out.

No Room

Scripture: Mary and Joseph had a hard time finding a place to stay to give birth to Jesus. (Luke 2:1-7)
This Game Teaches: Mary and Joseph ended up in a stable because all the hotel rooms were full.
Materials: A chair for each child (except for two)

63

Game: Have the children set up chairs in a circle. (Each child should have a chair except for two children.) Set the chairs far enough apart so that kids can sit in the chair and then run out and around the chairs.

Choose two children and say that they are Mary and Joseph. They are looking for a place to stay to give birth to baby Jesus.

Have Mary and Joseph walk around the outside of the circle. Have them tap the heads of each child sitting in a chair. When a child's head is tapped, he or she says, "No room!" After a bit, say, "Room scramble!"

When you say, "Room scramble," all the children sitting in chairs have to jump off their chairs and run across the circle to another chair. (No one is allowed to move over one or two chairs.) Meanwhile, Mary and Joseph can grab the first chair they find (thus, they usually get a chair). The last two people left become the new Mary and Joseph. Play the game again.

End the game by having the children all try to fit on the chairs. (They'll be squished.) Talk about how thankful you are that someone was kind enough to make more room for Mary and Joseph—even though all the rooms were filled.

So Much Wash

Scripture: Wash to become as clean as snow. (Psalm 51:1-10)
This Game Teaches: When God forgives us, it's like being cleansed on the inside.
Materials: Forty-two clothespins, twenty handkerchiefs (or rags or washcloths), two clotheslines that you secure from the beginning of the line to the end of the room (or use string, yarn, or thin rope)

Game: Before the game, hang up the two clotheslines so that the beginning of each clothesline will be close to the beginning point of each team and the end will extend across the room. (The clotheslines should be set up parallel to each other.) Mark the halfway point of each clothesline with a clothespin.

Form two teams of an equal number of players. If you have an odd number of children, have one team choose one child who will go twice.

Have the children form two lines. Give the first and third person in each line ten clothespins. Give the second and fourth person in each line five handkerchiefs (or rags or washcloths).

Say, "Psalm 51 is a psalm about forgiveness. It says when God forgives our sins, it's like God washes us on the inside and makes us cleaner than snow. We're going to play a game about washing."

Explain that when you say "Go," the first two children in each line will start at the beginning of their team's clothesline. The one will hold up a handkerchief (or rag or washcloth) while the other

team member places two clothespins on it (one on each end) to secure the handkerchief to the line. Once they have successfully hung up one handkerchief, they then must hang up the next one right next to the first one and continue this until all five are hanging up side by side.

After they have hung up the five, then they must remove the clothespins from the first four handkerchiefs and continue hanging the handkerchiefs on the clothesline, using the fifth hanging handkerchief as a place saver of where they go from there. Once they get to the halfway point (where a clothespin is marked on the clothesline), they can yell "Go" to the next couple in line who can start hanging handkerchiefs in the same manner.

Little by little, the groups of two will make their way to the end of the clothesline. Once one group gets to the end, they remove all the handkerchiefs and clothespins from their set and run back to their team to give the next two players their handkerchiefs and clothespins so that they can get started. See which team finishes first.

End the game by saying, "We wash ourselves on the outside when we shower and take baths. God washes us on the inside by forgiving our sins."

Bonus Idea

Instead of having teams work in pairs, have teammates spread out along the line of their team's clothesline. Have the first person in line hang up a handkerchief while the second takes it down and hands it to the third who hangs it up in front of him or her (and continues passing the handkerchief down the line in this manner). Once the second player starts taking down the first handkerchief, the first player can grab another handkerchief and two clothespins and begin pinning the second one to the line. See how long it can take to move all the handkerchiefs down the clothesline.

Knowing the Scriptures

Scripture: Apollos knew the scriptures well. (Acts 18:24-28)
This Game Teaches: Learning the scriptures well can help you in your Christian life.
Materials: Two die, two pieces of paper, two pencils, and two Bibles

65

Game: Tell the children about the story of Apollos in Acts 18:24-28. Explain that knowing the Bible well can help you in your Christian life.

Form two teams of about an equal number of players. If you have an odd number of children, it's okay if one team has one fewer player.

Have the children from each team sit together. Give each team a die, a piece of paper, and a pencil. Ask for each team to designate a scribe who will write things down.

Once teams have chosen a scribe, have the scribe make three large areas on the front of the paper numbered one, two, and three; and three large areas on the back of the paper numbered four, five, and six. Have the scribes write these instructions next to each number on their paper:

      1 = A book in the Old Testament
      2 = A place in the Bible (such as a city, country, or area)
      3 = A person in the Old Testament
      4 = A book in the New Testament
      5 = A story in the Bible
      6 = A person in the New Testament

Ask for another volunteer from each group. Give that person the die. Explain that teams will go around the circle clockwise. When you say, "Go," the first person will roll the die. Whatever number he or she gets, have the scribe interpret it. For example, if the person rolls a four, the scribe says, "A book in the New Testament."

The person must then name a book in the New Testament. The scribe writes that person's answer in the area under number four on the paper. If the person doesn't know, the person says, "pass," and hands the die to the next person.

The goal of the game is to get as many correct answers written on the sheet as possible. The scribe can also tell the team when duplicate answers are given since they do not count. (When it's the scribe's turn to play, have the player next to him or her be the scribe for that turn.)

Play for about five minutes. At the end of the game, talk about what the teams wrote on their sheets. Applaud them for what they correctly identified.

End the game by giving each team a Bible. Have the children look at the table of contents for the Old Testament and New Testament. Ask what surprises they see. Say, "The Bible is full of great stories, information, and advice. The more we learn, the better Christians we'll be."

Bonus Idea

To make the game more of a group effort, ask for one person to be the scribe. Post that person at a chalkboard, whiteboard, or poster board. Instead of each team having individual scribes, the one scribe records things as a whole group. Although kids still play as two teams, their choices become fewer since they can't duplicate the answers from the other group.

A Plague of Locusts

Scripture: God sends a plague of locusts when the Egyptians will not let God's people go. (Exodus 10:1-20)

This Game Teaches: Plagues were terrible events.

Materials: Two old men's shirts (ask people in your congregation for donations if you don't have any), lots of clothespins

66

Game: Form two teams of an equal number of players. If you have an odd number of children, have the extra child be the locust buzzer.

Have each group choose one person to be "It." Give that person an old man's shirt to put on. Have the child just have the shirt draped on. Do not button it or tuck it in. Give each team a large pile of clothespins.

Say, "In Exodus 10:1-20, the Egyptians would not let God's people go. So God sent a plague of locusts. The person wearing the shirt is your bad-guy Egyptian. Each of your clothespins is a locust. When I tell you to start, begin pinning clothespins to the Egyptian's shirt. Do this carefully. I don't want any pinched fingers. Hang the clothespin locusts everywhere and place them on as quickly and as safely as you can."

If you have an extra child, have this child run around the two groups saying, "Buzz. Buzz."

Begin the game. See how quickly the teams can cover their teammate with clothespins.

End the game by having the two children wearing the clothespin-covered shirts model their locust-covered shirts. Ask these two volunteers what it felt like to have everyone hanging clothespins on them.

Say, "The plagues were terrible events. It's good to be on God's side and to follow God."

Love Your Neighbor

Scripture: Love your neighbor as yourself. (Mark 12:28-31)
This Game Teaches: We are to love each other.
Materials: A chair for each child

67

Game: Have the children form a circle with their chairs. Make sure there is enough room between each chair so that it's easy to get up and switch chairs. Have one child remove the chair from the group and stand in the middle of the circle.

Read aloud Mark 12:28-31. Say, "We're going to play a game called 'Love Your Neighbor.' Before we begin the game, we're going to practice so that you can get used to the game."

Explain that you will ask a child this question: Do you love your neighbor? If that child says no, the two children on either side of that child must get up and switch seats. The problem, however, is that the child in the middle can grab one of the seats, which would leave one of the other children in the middle.

The child also can say yes to the question but give an exception. For example, "Yes, I love my neighbor, except for those wearing brown shoes." Any child wearing brown shoes must then get up and switch chairs. Again, the child in the middle can grab one of the seats.

Try the game with a couple of kids. Then play the game. Be intentional about asking a different child each time so that each child gets at least one turn.

End the game by having the children put their chairs away. Then have them form a circle. This time when you ask, "Do you love your neighbor?" say, "Yes, we love everybody." Then have the group do a group hug.

Who's the Leader?

Scripture: King Nebuchadnezzar orders people to worship a gold statue, but Daniel and his friends say no. They say people should worship only God. (Daniel 3:1-18)
This Game Teaches: A lot of people like to be the leader.
Materials: None

68

Game: Tell the story about King Nebuchadnezzar and Daniel from Daniel 3:1-18. Ask for a volunteer. Have the volunteer leave the room.

Ask for another volunteer to be the leader. When the other volunteer comes in the room, watch the room's leader. He or she will do some kind of action, which everyone must copy. For example, the leader might lift up his or her foot and look at the bottom of his or her shoe. Or the leader might start laughing. Or the leader might start clapping his or her hands.

Explain that you want to make this tricky because the volunteer who is outside needs to guess who the leader is. Encourage kids to not look at the leader all the time and try to conceal who is the leader.

Leave the room. Briefly explain the game to the child who is outside. Then enter the room with the child. See how long it takes

the child to figure out who the leader is.

Once the child figures it out, ask for two more volunteers: one to leave the room and one to be the new leader in the room.

End the game by asking who the leader was during Daniel's time. Then pray, "Thank you, God, for always being our leader. Amen."

Gather the Harvest

Scripture: Gather the harvest of your fields, and give the extras to the poor. (Leviticus 19:9-10)

This Game Teaches: Work hard and help the poor.

Materials: Sixteen ping-pong balls, an empty egg carton with the cover torn off, and an offering plate

69

Game: Say, "In the book of Leviticus, God says that it's good to work hard. When you're a farmer, working hard means harvesting your fields, bringing in the eggs from the chickens, and milking the cows. Let's play a game as if we're farmers."

Place an empty egg carton in the middle of the playing area. Have children surround the egg carton, standing about five feet away. Give each child a ping-pong ball.

Say, "When I say, 'Go,' try to bounce your ping-pong ball so that it lands in the egg carton. If you miss, grab another ping-pong ball. As a group, let's see how long it takes for us to fill this egg carton with a dozen ping-pong balls."

Play the game. Once the egg carton is full, the kids will notice there are four extra ping-pong balls.

End the game by saying, "In Leviticus, God said it's good to work hard, and God said it is important to give. In the Bible, farmers harvested the land and gave the leftovers to the poor. Now let's take these four ping-pong balls and bounce them into an offering plate."

Links of Love

Scripture: The power of love. (1 Corinthians 13)
This Game Teaches: We can love each other in many different, concrete ways.
Materials: 8 1/2 x 11 construction paper in red (six pieces), white (six pieces), and pink (six pieces), a paper cutter (or scissors), two staplers, masking tape, markers, three pieces of yellow paper, three pieces of orange paper

Game: Before you play the game, cut the construction paper into one-inch-wide strips. (You'll be able to make eight strips from each piece of 8 1/2 x 11 piece of paper.) With the yellow and orange paper, make signs using markers. You want to have one yellow and one orange sign that says "Family," another that says "Friends," and another that says "Poor." Hang the yellow signs on one side of the room, and hang the orange signs on the other side of the room.

Create a red link from one of the pieces of red construction paper by folding it into a loop and stapling it. Using masking tape, hang the red loop on the yellow paper that says Family. Make another red loop to hang on the orange Family paper.

Create two pink links. Hang one on the yellow Friends paper and the other on the orange Friends paper. Then create two white links. Hang one on the yellow Poor paper and the other on the orange Poor paper.

On a table, make a pile of the red strips, pink strips, and white strips. (Separate them so that they won't easily get mixed up during the game. If you have an extra child, he or she can monitor this and straighten the piles.) Make a pile of markers.

Form two teams of an equal number of players. If you have an odd number of children, have the extra child help keep the supplies in order during the game. Give each team a stapler.

Say, "First Corinthians 13 tells us all about love. We're going to play a game about love." Designate which team is the yellow team and which is the orange team.

Say, "When I tell you to start, begin writing concrete ways you can love your family on the red strips, your friends on the pink strips, and the poor on the white strips. Then use the stapler to attach each link to the link on your colored poster. For example, you could write on a red strip about taking out the garbage or smiling at your sister."

Ask the kids if they have any questions. Then play the game. See which team can make the longest chains.

End the game by celebrating the many ways kids identified how to love others. Read some of the examples from the paper chain. (Skip ones that don't fit.) Then connect the chains and hang the combined chain around your room.

Bonus Idea

Have each child make one colored link with an idea they want to do in the coming week. For example, they might want to invite a friend over to play and write that idea on a pink strip. Then make the link into a bracelet that they wear home.

Healing the Lame

Scripture: Jesus heals the lame. (John 5:1-18)
This Game Teaches: We should help each other.
Materials: Eighteen pencils of one color and two pencils of a different color (the pencils do not need to be sharpened)

Game: Set up the pencils for a two-team relay. (Each team will have ten pencils, nine of one color and one of another color.) Lay the pencils in a row about one foot apart. (It should look like a ladder with only steps once you're finished.) Make sure the different colored pencil is the pencil closest to the team. Set this up for two teams.

71

Form two teams of an equal number of players. If you have an odd number of children, have one team choose one child who will go twice.

Have the children form two lines. Have the lines stationed about ten feet away from the first pencil. Say, "In John 5, Jesus healed the lame. We're going to play a game where we carry the lame toward

us. Each team has ten lame people, represented by pencils. When I tell you to start, the first person in line runs up to the pencil and then hops over each pencil until you get to the last pencil. Pick up the last pencil and hop back over the pencils. Place the pencil you picked up about six inches to a foot in front of the different colored pencil. When you get back to your team, the second player will do the same thing, although the first pencil is now a different pencil than before. Each player will pick up the last pencil and move it to the front of the line. The first team to get all their pencils moved so that the different colored pencil is back to being first will be the winner."

Play the game. As the game gets close to finishing, the team may need to back up, since the row of pencils will be moving toward them.

End the game by having the children scoop up all their pencils. Give each child a pencil. Pray, "Help us, God, to help those who need our help. Amen."

Bonus Idea

Instead of moving the pencils, you could have a bucket at the beginning of each line. As each child carries a pencil, he or she can drop the pencil into the bucket as he or she tags the next person in line.

Scramble to Home

Scripture: Jesus tells of a time when everyone will be scattered to their own home and Jesus will be left alone. (John 16:31-33)

This Game Teaches: Sometimes when we move around, we get left out.

Materials: A stack of 8 1/2 x 11 paper

Game: Read aloud John 16:31-33. Explain that you're going to play a game about people being scattered about and one being left alone.

Form groups of five. (It's okay if some groups have four or six.) If you have only six kids present, have the entire group play together.

For each group, give a piece of paper to each child except for one. Have the four children with the paper create an imaginary box around the child about two or three feet away. Ask each child to place a piece of paper on the ground.

Say, "The person in the middle wants to go home, but the only people who have a home are those who are standing on a piece of paper. When I call out, 'Go!' everyone has to run to a different home. The child in the middle also gets to run and try to find a home before another child does. The trick, however, is that only one child can stand on one piece of paper. The child who gets left out has to stand in the middle."

Play the game a few times.

End the game by asking questions such as these:
- How did it feel to get stuck in the middle? Why?
- Which made your heart beat faster: being on a piece of paper and knowing you need to scramble to another piece of paper or being in the middle? Why?
- Who are the people today who don't have a home? How can we help them?

Clean on the Inside and Out

Scripture: People need to ask for forgiveness often. (Hebrews 10:1-3)
This Game Teaches: It's good to admit when we've sinned.
Materials: Shaving cream, two rolls of paper towels, two wastebaskets, markers, paper for each child

Game: Form two teams of an equal number of players. If you have an odd number of children, have one child monitor the wastebaskets and pick up trash that gets missed.

Have the children on each team sit in a circle. Ask for two volunteers for each team. One volunteer will have shaving cream applied to his or her face. The other volunteer will be the one to clean off the shaving cream. As the adult, put shaving cream on the faces of the two teams' volunteers (one face for each team). Station the other volunteer next to the child with shaving cream and place a wastebasket next to him or her. Have the child with the shaving cream close his or her eyes.

Give the child on the other side of the child

with shaving cream a roll of paper towels. Say, "When I tell you to start, the child with the paper towels will tear off one paper towel and pass it to the person next to him or her who does not have shaving cream. Pass the paper towel as quickly as you can around the circle. When the other volunteer without shaving cream gets the paper towel, he or she gets one swipe to clean off the shaving cream before throwing away the paper towel. Once the paper towel is in the wastebasket, the child holding the paper towels can tear off another sheet and send it around the circle."

See how many paper towels it takes to clear off all the shaving cream. Note that the ending paper towels will be used more carefully since the volunteers will be trying to erase all the shaving cream.

End the game by having the children with shaving cream wash up. Then gather the group together. Give each child a piece of paper and a marker.

Say, "We just played a game about cleaning faces. God says it's important that we clean ourselves on the inside as well. That means to clean us from sin. On the piece of paper, write one bad thing you have done. Don't show it to anyone, and no one will see it. Be honest. When you're finished, fold your paper in half."

Give children time to do this. Once everyone has finished, have children form circles around the two wastebaskets. Say, "God forgives your sins. We're going to go around the circle and when it's your turn, rip up your paper and drop it in the wastebasket while you say, 'God forgives my sin.' "

Bonus Idea

Instead of having players pass the paper towels with their hands, have them take off their socks and shoes and lie on their backs. Have them pass the paper towel with their toes.

Where in the Bible?

Scripture: The Bible has sixty-six books in it. (The Old Testament has thirty-nine books. The New Testament has twenty-seven books.)
This Game Teaches: There is a lot to learn about the Bible.
Materials: Two large pieces of paper, a new pad of 3-inch by 3-inch sticky notes, markers, masking tape

74

Game: Before you play the game, label one large piece of paper "Old Testament." Hang it on the wall. Label the other large piece of paper "New Testament." Hang it on the same wall but farther away.

Using a Bible's table of contents, label each 3-inch by 3-inch sticky note with one book of the Bible. (You will use sixty-six sticky notes since there are sixty-six books in the Bible.) Once you finish, place these sticky notes on a table or hang them on another wall. (Make sure you mix up the books of the Bible so that you have books from the Old Testament and New Testament mixed together.)

Say, "The Bible has sixty-six books. Do you know which belong in the Old Testament and which belong in the New Testament? When I tell you to start, pick up a sticky note and place it either under Old Testament or New Testament. Then find another sticky note and do the same. Keep going until all the sticky notes are on this wall." Point to the wall that has the Old and New Testament labels.

Have children play the game. When they finish, create two teams. Post one at the Old Testament space and the other at the New Testament space. Have each team analyze each sticky note and decide whether it's in the right place or not.

End the game by going through the sixty-six books of the Bible. See how the kids did. Congratulate them on the ones they got right.

The Twelve

Scripture: Twelve disciples followed Jesus. (Mark 3:16-19)
This Game Teaches: Who the twelve disciples are.
Materials: A piece of 8 1/2 x 11 paper for each child, marker, masking tape, chalkboard and chalk (or white board with white board markers or poster board)

Game: Before you play the game, write the name of the twelve disciples (and any description in parenthesis) on pieces of paper. (Write one disciple's name on each paper.) The names are: Peter (also known as Simon and Andrew's brother), Andrew (Peter's brother), James (son of Zebedee and John's brother), John (son of Zebedee and James' brother), Philip, Bartholomew, Thomas (the doubter), Matthew (the tax collector), James (son of Alphaeus), Thaddaeus, Simon the Patriot, and Judas Iscariot (the betrayer).

On a chalkboard, write these questions:

- Am I someone's brother?
- Am I someone's son?
- Does my name start with the letter J?
- Does my name start with the letter P?
- Does my name start with the letter T?

List the names of the twelve along with the info in parenthesis on the chalkboard as well since children will be familiar with a few of the disciples but not all of them.

Say, "The Bible talks about twelve disciples following Jesus. I'm going to hang one of the disciple's names on your back. You will not know what it is, but everyone else will. When I tell you to start, pair up with another child and ask one of the questions on the chalkboard. Then meet up with another child and ask another question. Continue until you've asked all the questions on the board. You may not guess a name of a disciple. That will come later. As you're asking the questions, try to figure out who you could be."

If you have fewer than twelve children, hang up the extra

disciple names on the chalkboard so that the kids know who has already been identified. If you have more than twelve children, play with twelve children at a time.

Have the children stand in a parallel line with their backs toward you. Hang one disciple name on each child's back with masking tape. Make sure none of the children see who they have posted on their backs.

Play the game. When children have had a chance to ask all the questions, bring the group together.

Ask, "Who knows who they are?" (Some will have a good idea; others may not.) Ask one of the children who claims to know who they are to stand and turn around so everyone can read the name on his or her back. Then have the child name who he or she is.

If the child is correct, say so. Place an X next to the disciple's name on the list on the chalkboard. If the child is incorrect, say so. Have the child sit down and wait until others have had a turn. Continue until everyone has figured out who she or he is.

End the game by having the children vote on who's the most famous disciple (in order). Talk about why some disciples are more famous than others.

Bonus Idea

To help the children learn more about the twelve disciples, use a Bible dictionary or a Bible concordance to look up the names of each of the disciples. Assign each child a different disciple to learn about. (If you have more than twelve kids, you can create pairs or small groups. If you have fewer than twelve kids, you can assign two disciples per child.) Have kids share what they learned about their disciple.

Note

The scripture passages in Mark 3:16-19 and Matthew 10:1-4 list the same names for the twelve disciples. If you wish, you may want to use the scripture passages in Luke 6:13-16 or Acts 1:13, which have the same twelve names except for one. In Luke and in Acts, Thaddaeus does not appear as a disciple, but Judas the son of James, does.

Section 4

Great Games for
MIXED GRADES (K-6)

Sometimes you have a couple of five-year-olds, a seven-year-old, a ten-year-old, and a twelve-year-old. That's a total of five children, and you group them together for Christian education and other events.

Grouping children of different ages will work as long as you're strategic about programming for a wide range of ages. Kindergartners are vastly different from sixth-graders, and keeping children from all ages engaged can be a trick. The problem, however, is that most curriculum is geared for a specific age group—or for a small range of ages.

The twenty-six games in this section are easy for kindergartners but also have elements to them that keep older children enthused. Team up older children with younger children whenever a game requires reading or another ability that can be difficult for the younger children. Talk with older children about the importance of buddies, and how older buddies can help younger buddies.

Focus on building community. Your younger children will love knowing the names of the older children, and your older children will be surprised by how good it feels when a young child runs up to them after worship to say hello.

Consider using these games not only for education classes but also for times when you provide childcare for church events. Although children do like free play for a certain period of time, they also like structure. Use these games to create a fun structure that can help them learn more about the Bible, faith, and each other.

Amazing Kids

Scripture: God knows each one of us. (Psalm 139:13-16)
This Game Teaches: Every single person is amazing in God's eyes.
Materials: Before you play this game, get one bucket (or a box). Get a sticky nametag, marker, and an index card for each player.

Game: Give each player a sticky nametag, a marker, and an index card. Have each person clearly print his or her name on the nametag and stick it on his or her chest. (You or the older children may need to assist some of the younger children.) Then have each person clearly print his or her name on the index card and place it in a bucket.

Ask someone to mix all the index cards inside of the bucket (or box). Ask each person to choose one index card. If someone chooses his or her own name, have that person return the index card to the bucket and choose another name. Tell players not to let anyone see the name they pulled from the bucket. (If the kids don't know each other well, have them quietly walk around the room and make note of who matches the name on their index card without letting anyone know who they have. This game can also be a helpful get-to-know-you game.)

Have the children sit in a circle. Ask for a

volunteer to start. Have that person give one clue about the person he or she chose from the bucket. For example, a person can say, "This person is a boy (or a girl)." (Other clues might include hair color, eye color, clothing color, or whether or not the person wears glasses.) Have the other children raise their hands. The chosen child can make one guess. If the guess is wrong, the child gives a different clue, and children raise their hands again. Continue until the right person is guessed. Then go to the next child to guess who he or she has picked from the bucket.

After the game ends, say: "God thinks each one of you is amazing. God made each of us unique. Some of us have black hair. Some have brown hair. Others are blond. God loves each one of us just the way we are."

Yummy Food

Scripture: Do not worry. God gives us food to eat. (Luke 12:22-31)
This Game Teaches: God has given us a large variety of food to eat.
Materials: None

Game: Ask for two volunteers. Have one volunteer be the "eater" and the other be the main ingredient in the meal.

Have all the children line up behind the volunteer who is the main ingredient in the meal. Say, "God gives us a lot of good food. This person *(point to the first person in line)* is the bread. When I say go, I want the person behind him or her to name an ingredient in a sandwich. Then the third person will name another ingredient. We'll keep going until the end of the line."

Say, "Go," and listen to the sandwich that the kids create. Then say, "This person here is very hungry. *(Point to the other volunteer, who is the 'eater.')* When I say, 'Run,' run around the room in your line and hold out your hand. The eater will run in the opposite direction. He or she will hit each one of your hands and make eating noises."

When the kids finish, play the game again but choose different volunteers. Instead of naming ingredients in a sandwich, name ingredients in a salad, soup, leftovers, or a dessert.

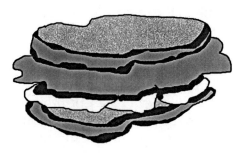

End the game by having the children form a circle and hold hands. Say, "God gives us many good foods. And when we all finish eating, we all say . . . *(pause)*." Then as a group lift your hands over your head and say "Amen" as you drop your hands together.

Faith, Hope, and Love

Scripture: Of faith, hope, and love, the greatest is love. (1 Corinthians 13:1-13)
This Game Teaches: God calls us to have faith, hope, and love.
Materials: Two books, two brooms, and two umbrellas

78

Game: Form two teams of an equal number of players. If you have an odd number of children, have one team choose one child who will go twice.

Have the children form two lines. Give the first person in each line a book, a broom, and an umbrella. Ask the children to open the umbrella.

Have one child demonstrate. Have the child place the book on his or her head, hold the broom in one hand, and hold the umbrella in the other hand. The child then needs to balance all three and walk across the room to a designated point. (Place a chair or create a line with masking tape on the floor.) The child then needs to turn around and walk back to the line, carefully handing everything to the next player who can then start to walk, once he or she has everything balanced.

Explain that if anyone drops anything, the person must stop, run back to the beginning of the line and start over.

Start the game. Have a race between the two teams.

End the game by having the children sit. Place the book on your head. Say, "First Corinthians 13 talks about how important it is to love. We need to love each other very much. First Corinthians 13 also says we need to have faith. (*Have someone hand you a broom while you balance the book on your head.*) The scripture also says we need hope. *(Have someone hand you the open umbrella.)* God calls us to do a lot: to have faith, to have hope, and to love. We can do all this when we think about them, and when we mess up, *(drop something)*, we can start over *(pick up the item)* and have faith, hope, and love again."

Bonus Idea

Have children take off their socks and shoes. Have them lie on their backs in a single line and raise their feet into the air. Place one book on the bottom of the first person's feet. Have children pass the book (carefully) down the line with their feet. See how far they can get without dropping it.

Give as Much as You Can

Scripture: Your heart will be where your riches are. Give to the poor. (Luke 12:33-34)

This Game Teaches: Give as much as you can.

Materials: Two buckets, a bunch of bouncy balls or ping-pong balls, a clock or watch that can measure seconds

79

Game: Form two teams of an equal number of players. If you have an odd number of children, have one team choose one child who will go twice.

Have the children form two lines. Give each child a bouncy or ping-pong ball. Create a stash of more bouncy or ping-pong balls at the front of the line for each team. Place a bucket about three feet in front of the first person in each line.

Explain that the goal is to get as many bouncy (or ping-pong) balls into your team's bucket within two minutes. Say that when you say "Go," the first person in each line will either throw or bounce the ball toward the bucket. If the ball gets in, the person runs to the back of the line and the second person tries. If you miss, run after the ball while the second person tries to throw the ball. (Yes, this game will get crazy with a lot of bouncy balls and running children, but that's part of what makes it fun.)

After two minutes, call stop. Count the number of balls in each bucket. Most likely there will not be many in either bucket. Play the game again. (The children will gradually get the feel of what it takes to get a ball into the bucket.)

End the game by having the children place all the balls into one bucket. Have the group count the balls. Read aloud Luke 12:33-34 and say how it's better to give than to receive.

Keep Going

Scripture: Live the Christian life. (Philippians 1:27-30)
This Game Teaches: Keep going—no matter what.
Materials: Two sets of bubble solution and wands

Game: Form two teams of an equal number of players. If you have an odd number of children, have one team choose one child who will go twice.

Have the children form two lines. Give the child at the front of each line a container with bubble solution in it and a wand. Have one child demonstrate by blowing a bubble, catching a bubble on the wand, and walking with the bubble.

Mark a turnaround point where children will walk to and turn around. (Mark it with a chair or with masking tape on the ground.) Explain that when you say, "Go," the first child in each line will blow a bubble, catch it on the wand, and begin to walk once the bubble is on the wand. If the bubble breaks, the child needs to stop, blow another bubble and not move forward until the bubble is resting on the wand. Each child needs to walk to the turnaround point and come back to the team and hand off the bubble solution and wand to the next player in line.

Once the teams finish, end the game by having the children sit. Say, "Philippians 1:27-30 tells us to live a good Christian life. That's like walking with a bubble on a wand. Sometimes, times get tough and the bubble breaks. That's why it's important to keep trying so that we can keep going."

Bonus Idea

Instead of catching the bubble on the wand, blow the bubble as you walk.

Doing More Together

Scripture: The people work together to complete the Holy Tent, and Moses blesses them. (Exodus 39:32-43)

This Game Teaches: We can do more when we work together.

Materials: One bucket, a bunch of bouncy (or ping-pong) balls, a piece of chalk (if you play this outside) or masking tape (if you play this inside)

81

Game: Place a bucket on the floor (if you're playing inside) or on the concrete (if you're playing outside). Draw a circle with chalk around the bucket that's about two feet wider than the bucket. (If you're playing inside, make a box on the floor with masking tape.)

Have the children gather about five feet away from the bucket. Explain that the masking tape (or chalk) marks a no-entry zone. No one can step inside that line. Say that one child will throw the ball

and try to have it bounce once before it gets into the bucket. If the ball misses, everyone can run to the ball. As soon as someone picks up the ball, he or she shouts, "Got it!" and everyone freezes. Children cannot move, but they can toss the ball to another player who may be more strategically positioned to bounce the ball once before getting it into the bucket. If the ball misses, the children can move again.

Once the children succeed at getting the ball into the bucket, they run back to where they started the game. Another child can then throw a ball and start the game again. Continue until all the balls are in the bucket.

End the game by briefly telling the story of Exodus 39:32-43 where all the people worked together to build a Holy Tent. Moses was so pleased with how they worked together, he blessed them. Bless the children for playing well together.

More, More, More

Scripture: The parable of the rich fool who piles up riches. (Luke 12:13-21)
This Game Teaches: When you want more, it's hard to keep track of it all. You can spend all your time getting more and protecting what you have.
Materials: Lots of clothespins

82

Game: Give each child four clothespins. Have children clip the clothespins either to the bottom of their shirt (hanging out) or to the bottom of a sleeve.

Explain that when the game begins, children are to run around and try to steal clothespins off of someone else. When they steal a clothespin, they are to clip it to their sleeve or to the bottom of their shirt. The trick, however, is that they also want to guard their clothespins at the same time. The goal is to have the most clothespins at the end of the game.

Begin the game. Chaos will ensue.

End the game by reading aloud Luke 12:13-21. Say, "When we want more, we become greedy. We begin thinking of more, more, more instead of thinking about God. Instead, it's better to share what we have and to trust God to provide for our needs."

One, Two, Three— Thanks, Thanks, Thanks

Scripture: A prayer of thanksgiving. (Psalm 138)
This Game Teaches: We have much to be thankful for.
Materials: A ball for every two children

Game: Ask the children to each find a partner. If you have an extra child, create a group of three. Give each group a ball.

Say, "We have much to be thankful for. Face your partner and stand about two feet apart. Each time you throw the ball to your partner, name something you're thankful for. As you name things, count. For example: 1. God's love. 2. Good food. 3. Sunshine. See how many things you can name without dropping the ball. If you drop the ball, start over."

Play the game.

End the game by having the children stand in a circle and hold hands. Close with a prayer of gratitude where each child names one thing he or she is thankful for as you go around the circle.

Bonus Idea

Make the game more challenging by having the children take a step back every time they catch the ball.

Manna Madness

Scripture: People gather manna from the ground to eat. (Exodus 16)
This Game Teaches: God always provides.
Materials: Two large bags of cotton balls, two laundry baskets

84

Game: Form two teams of an equal number of players. If you have an odd number of children, have one set up the game and then watch it while it's being played.

Have the two teams stand at opposite corners of the room. Have your extra child (or you can do this if you have an even number of children) place a laundry basket next to each team and spread out the cotton balls from the two bags onto the floor or ground between the two teams.

Say, "In Exodus 16, God fed the people by placing manna on the ground. Manna was white, and people had to pick up the manna. When I say 'Go,' run out and grab as many cotton balls as you can. Carry them back to your laundry basket and dump them in. The team with the most cotton balls at the end is the winner."

Play the game. Most likely, cotton balls will be flying all over since kids will try to grab and carry more than they can handle. At the end, have each team count the cotton balls.

End the game by saying, "God always takes care of us. In Exodus 16, the people were hungry and didn't know where they would find food. God provided food for them."

Bonus Idea

Play the game without the laundry baskets and teams. See how many cotton balls each child can pick up and hold onto.

Cleaner and Whiter than Snow

Scripture: A prayer of forgiveness. (Psalm 51:1-10)
This Game Teaches: When God forgives us, it's like being cleansed on the inside.
Materials: Two buckets with water in them, two bars of soap

Game: Form two teams of an equal number of players. If you have an odd number of children, have one team choose one child who will go twice.

Have the children form two lines. Place each bucket of water about twenty feet in front of each line. Give the first child in each line a bar of soap.

Say, "When I tell you to go, run to the bucket, dip the soap in it, run back and give the soap to the next person in line. Then each person will do the same thing." Play the game. Keep an eye out for spills so that only the bars of soap—and not the children—are slipping.

End the game by reading aloud Psalm 51:1-10. Ask the children what it means to be forgiven and become whiter than snow.

Bonus Idea

If you have a warm day, play this game outside. Add two more buckets of water to the game. Place the additional buckets at the front of each line so that children dip the soap twice: when they're handed the soap and when they run out to the bucket twenty feet away.

Rainbow Run

Scripture: God sent a rainbow as a promise. (Genesis 9:8-17)
This Game Teaches: Color is everywhere.
Materials: None

86

Game: Have children line up at one end of the room. Ask for a volunteer. The volunteer stands in the middle of the room and will tag people during the game.

Say, "God sent a rainbow of many colors after the flood. The rainbow is a sign of the promise that God will never flood the earth again. We're going to play a game that has all the colors of the rainbow."

Explain that the volunteer will yell out a color. If anyone is wearing that color (anywhere as clothing, shoes, or socks), those children need to run into the middle and look for something of the same color to touch before they are tagged. For example, if the volunteer calls blue, children wearing blue need to run out and touch a blue chair, a blue poster, a blue tissue box, or something else that is blue. Anyone who is tagged before finding the color must stand at the opposite end of the room until the game is over.

Once everyone is safe or tagged, have them all return to starting positions. Have the volunteer name another color and play the game again.

End the game by having children line up in the order of the colors of the rainbow (according to the colors they're wearing): red, orange, yellow, green, blue, and purple.

Bonus Idea

To give the game more variety, have the first person tagged become the new volunteer who names colors.

Wolves and Sheep

Scripture: Good shepherds protect sheep from the wolves. (John 10:7-21)

This Game Teaches: It's good to protect others from harm. Jesus is the ultimate shepherd and protector.

Materials: None

Game: Identify how many children you have playing. If you have six or fewer, designate one child to be the wolf, two to be the shepherds, and the rest to be the sheep. If you have seven or more children, have two wolves. If you have ten or more, have two wolves, four shepherds, and the rest sheep. If you have a lot of children, make sure you have a ratio of shepherds to sheep of no more than three sheep to every two shepherds.

Tell the story of Jesus the Good Shepherd or read aloud the scripture in John 10:7-21.

Explain that you'll now play the game. Designate which children are wolves, shepherds, and sheep. Have two children who are shepherds demonstrate how they can protect sheep by joining hands and having the sheep standing between them. (They cannot have more than three sheep inside their arms.) Explain that when

you say, "Go," the wolf will try to tag a sheep, and shepherds can protect the sheep for a count of five. Have the children spread out. Begin the game.

End the game by having the children howl like wolves or baa like sheep.

Gather Quickly

Scripture: Ruth gathers grain. (Ruth 2:1-7)
This Game Teaches: At harvest time, it's important to work hard and gather the grain.
Materials: A straw and paper cup for each child, lots of small pieces of paper (about 1 inch by 1 inch)

88

Game: Before the game, cut paper into 1-inch by 1-inch squares. (The size doesn't need to be exact, but the pieces need to be small. Consider using a paper cutter to cut a lot of pieces quickly.)

Give each child ten pieces of paper, a straw, and a paper cup. Have kids spread out their ten pieces of paper.

Explain that a woman named Ruth in the Bible went to work in the fields. At harvest time, she gathered grain. For this game, the pieces of paper are the grain. The straw is the way to transport the grain, and the cup will hold the grain.

Ask one child to demonstrate using the straw to pick up a piece of paper and place it in the cup without using his or her hands. (The child will need to suck in air and make sure the entire hole of the straw sits on the paper to create enough suction to pick it up.) After the demonstration, have the child empty the cup so everyone's paper pieces are on the table.

Play the game. See who can pick up all ten pieces of paper the fastest.

End the game by talking about the different ways we gather things today (since few people farm). Examples could include gathering stuff from around the home to clean it, gathering leaves in the fall to bag them, gathering carrots from the garden, and so on.

Bonus Idea

Play this game by forming two teams where everyone has a straw. Give ten pieces of paper to the first child in each line. Give one paper cup to the last child in each line. Have a race to see which team can pass the ten pieces of paper (by using straws only) from player to player until the end of the line.

A Big, Big World

Scripture: Christ died for the sins of the whole world. (1 John 2:1-6)
This Game Teaches: Everybody in the world counts.
Materials: Lots of paper clips, a map or globe of the world

89

Game: Read aloud 1 John 2:1-6, emphasizing verse two and how Christ came to forgive the sins of everyone in the world.

Give each child a pile of paper clips. Have a world map or globe of the world available for the children to use to identify countries.

Before you play the game, identify how many children you have. If you have more than eight, create small groups of five or six to do this game. Otherwise if your group has eight children or fewer, do the game together.

To play the game, have the children start on one continent. You may want to start them with North America since they're most familiar with that continent. Have one child pick up a paper clip and name one country on that continent (such as the United States). Then go around the circle and ask the next child to name another country on that same continent (such as Canada). Have that child clip his or her paper clip to the first child's paper clip. (If children struggle with this at first, demonstrate how to link paper clips.) Encourage children to use the world map or globe to identify a country.

Continue until all the countries on one continent are named. Then move to a nearby continent. (Keep track of the continents since you'll visit every continent for this game.)

Play the game. As children identify more countries, the paper clip chain will grow longer and longer.

End the game after you've visited all the countries. You should have a very long chain. Talk about how long your chain would be if you made one person by person. (The world currently has more than six billion people living on it.) Close with a prayer, thanking God for sending Christ to die for all of our sins.

Bonus Idea

Create a paper clip chain to symbolize other large numbers, such as the number of people who die each day from starvation or the number of children who are homeless in America.

Seek and Find

Scripture: Ask and you will receive. Seek and you will find. Knock and the door will be open to you. (Matthew 7:7-12)
This Game Teaches: Ask and seek for what you want.
Materials: Two decks of playing cards

90 **Game:** Before you play this game, remove cards from one deck equal to the number of children who will be playing the game. If you're not sure, estimate more than what you need. For example, if you usually have six kids, plan on having eight.

Once you pull the number of cards from one deck, find the identical card in the second deck. (For example, if you will have a two of hearts from each set.) Make sure you have an identical match for each card.

Hide one set of the cards around your playing area (so that you have all the identical matches in your hand). If you have a lot of older children, hide them more than if you have a lot of younger children.

To play the game, give each child one playing card from your hand. Read aloud Matthew 7:7-12. Say that when you start the game, each child is to hunt for a matching card.

Play the game. If all the children find their cards except for one or two, ask for all the players to help those who are struggling.

End the game by having the children place their pairs face up on the table. Say, "When we seek, we will find. When we ask questions, we'll get answers. When we knock, the door will be opened."

Bonus Idea

Create two teams of children. Hide all the cards in one deck. Have one team search for all the red cards while the other looks for all the black cards. As they find matches, have them place their matches face up on the table. See who can find all their cards first.

What's the Time, Mr. King?

Scripture: The king of Egypt chases God's people across the Red Sea. (Exodus 14)
This Game Teaches: A bad king tried to hurt God's people.
Materials: None

91

Game: Ask for a volunteer. Have that person stand about one-fourth of the way on a playing area. Have the rest of the children line up so that they're about three-fourths away from the volunteer.

Say, "In the Old Testament, there was a bad king in Egypt who was trying to hurt God's people. He had them in slavery, and Moses kept asking the king to let the people go. When the king said yes, the people were crossing the Red Sea. The king changed his mind and wanted the people back, so he chased them across the Red Sea."

Explain that you're playing the game. The volunteer is the bad king. Everyone else is part of God's people. Have the volunteer turn his or her back to the group.

Have the group ask, "What's the time, Mr. King?" The king then picks a number between one and twelve (like on a clock). Whatever number the king picks, the children need to take that many steps toward the king. Once the kids have moved, they ask the question again.

At some point, have the king say, "Time to capture you again!" The king then turns around and chases the kids, trying to tag them. The kids who make it back to the wall (or starting line) are safe. The first one tagged becomes the new king.

End the game by asking if anyone knows how the story of the Red Sea ends. (God's people get across safely, but then the waters close up and the king's army drowns.) Thank God in a prayer about how God always is with God's people and keeps them safe.

Bonus Idea

If you have a large group, consider having two volunteers (or three). Have one be the king who says the time, and the other volunteers can be part of the king's army who turn around the help the king chase the others.

Official Clothing

Scripture: The Lord anoints a new leader (Eliakim) by clothing him with official clothes. (Isaiah 22:20-23)

This Game Teaches: People in authority often wear official clothing.

Materials: Two pieces of 8 1/2 x 11 paper, robes, two belts, two caps, and two pairs of gloves or mittens

92

Game: Before the game, make one pile of one piece of paper (on the bottom of the pile), one robe, one belt, one cap, and one pair of gloves (or mittens) about twenty feet away from where you will have the children line up to play the game. Make another pile of the other items nearby so that the two teams can have a relay.

Form two teams of an equal number of players. If you have an odd number of children, have one team choose one child who will go twice.

Have the children form two lines. Say, "In Isaiah, God appointed a new leader and said he would wear an official robe and belt. We're going to play a game about wearing official clothing."

Explain that when you say, "Go," the first child in each line will run out to the team's pile and put on one piece of clothing from the pile. The child then runs back to the team while wearing the clothing piece. When the child reaches the line, he or she takes off the clothing piece. The second child puts it on

and runs out to the pile and adds a second piece of clothing. That child runs back, hands the two pieces of clothing to the next child in line. Each child continues the game, adding another piece of clothing.

If you have more children than pieces of clothing, the last players continue running out to the point where the pile is (it will be marked on the floor with a blank sheet of paper) and back. (The piece of paper will be the only item from the pile that will not be picked up.) Children will wear all the pieces of clothing while running and then pass them to the next child.

End the game when all the children have played the game. Then start a discussion about official clothing that certain professions wear. Ask questions about what your pastor wears, firefighters, doctors, police officers, delivery people, bakers, and other professionals who wear specific clothing.

Bonus Idea

Adapt this game to show what children wear during different seasons of the year. For example, in winter have children put on cap, scarf, gloves, boots, and winter coats. In summer, have children put on sunglasses, flip-flops (have them take off their socks and shoes and play the game barefoot), a beach towel (to drape over their shoulders), and sunscreen.

Lost and then Found

Scripture: Jesus tells parables about the lost sheep, the lost coin, and the lost son. (Luke 15)

This Game Teaches: Be happy with what you find.

    Materials: One quarter, a small stuffed sheep, and a small toy that is a boy

93

Game: Ask one child to read aloud the parable of the lost sheep (Luke 15:1-7). When the child finishes, show the children the small

stuffed sheep. Then ask for a volunteer. Have all the children leave the room except for the volunteer.

    Ask the volunteer to hide the sheep somewhere in the room. Then have the volunteer sit down.

    Invite the children back in the room. Tell them that there is a lost sheep hidden in the room. The trick, however, is that once they find it, they should not tell anyone. They should walk around the room a little bit more and then sit down near the volunteer. The last person standing is the next volunteer.

After you play the game, have another child read aloud the parable of the lost coin (Luke 15:8-10). Then play the game again with the quarter.

    The third time, have a child read aloud the parable of the lost son (Luke 15:11-32). Then play the game again with the toy boy.

    End the game by saying, "Jesus often spoke in parables. With these parables, Jesus said it was important to seek what was lost and then to rejoice when the lost was found."

A Joyful Splash

Scripture: Shout to God with cries of joy. (Psalm 47)
This Game Teaches: God wants us to have fun.
Materials: A warm or hot day (play this game outdoors), clothes that kids can get wet, a sponge for each child—and for yourself, four buckets of water

Game: Before the game, make sure parents know that the children will be playing outside and will get wet. Play this game on a warm or hot summer day. Fill four buckets with water and place them around a playing area.

Read aloud Psalm 47. Tell the children that God wants us to have fun sometimes and that you're going to play a fun game.

Give each child a sponge. Explain that this game is called "A Joyful Splash." Children are to dip their sponges into a water bucket and then throw their wet sponge at someone from the waist down. Once they've tossed their sponge, they can pick up their sponge and throw it at someone else. When their sponge loses too much water, they can refill their sponge by dipping it in one of the buckets.

94

Play the game. Be prepared to get wet. (The kids will come after you, too!)

End the game after everyone is drenched. Remove the sponges and the water (to ensure that someone doesn't keep playing). Run around and dry off.

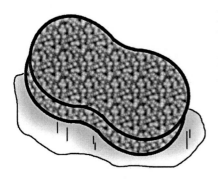

Bonus Idea

Play this game as sponge tag. Have one bucket of water available and only two sponges Ask for two volunteers to be "It." Give each volunteer a wet sponge. Have children run around the playing area. Volunteers try to tag them by hitting them (below the waist) with a wet sponge. After a few minutes, stop the game. Have the kids vote who is the wettest. The two wettest players become "It" for the next game.

Caught in Jail

Scripture: Paul and Silas are in jail. (Acts 16)
This Game Teaches: Some of God's followers were sent to jail, but God was always with them.
Materials: Two beanbags. (You can make your own by placing dried beans into one sock and tying the end of the sock so that beans stay secure in the sock.)

Game: Tell the story about Paul and Silas from Acts 16. Explain that you're going to play a game about jail. Ask for two volunteers. Say that one is Paul and the other is Silas. Have the two volunteers stand in the middle while the rest of the children form a circle around the volunteers.

Give a beanbag to two children in the circle. Explain that children will throw the beanbags across the circle to another player. If Paul or Silas intercepts the beanbag, then the person who threw it switches places. When you yell, "Earthquake," everyone runs around the room and falls down.

After an earthquake, pick two new children to be Paul and Silas. Play the game again.

End the game by having the children form a circle and hold hands. Pray, "Thank you, God, for Christians who are willing to go to jail for you, like Paul and Silas. Thank you for being with us—no matter where we are."

What a Whale!

Scripture: A whale swallows Jonah when he doesn't follow God. (Jonah 1)

This Game Teaches: It's important to obey God.

Materials: One piece of 8 1/2 x 11 white paper for each child, markers, and a die. (If you have more than ten kids present, you might want to have an extra die.)

96

Game: Before the game, write the following in large print on a piece of paper, poster board, chalkboard, or whiteboard:

1 = head
2 = body
3 = spout with water
4 = tail
5 = eye
6 = mouth

Give each child one piece of white paper and a marker. Briefly tell the story of Jonah from Jonah 1. Say that you're going to play a game about the whale that swallowed Jonah.

Explain that each child will take a turn rolling the die. (If you have more than ten kids present, create two groups of kids with each group having a die. That way kids won't have to wait so long for another turn.)

Whatever number the child gets on the die, that is what he or she should draw on the paper. For example, if a child rolls a five, the child should draw an eye. Explain that the goal is to get one of each number so that by the end, the child will have drawn the whale that swallowed Jonah.

If a child rolls the die and gets a number he or she got before, the child loses a turn and has to wait to roll the die next time.

Enjoy the funny whales that emerge from the drawings. (Drawing a whale in this way will be tricky—and will often be hilarious.) Encourage children to laugh at what develops.

End the game once all the children have finished their drawings. Say, "Even though God was not happy with Jonah, God was still with Jonah—even in the belly of the whale."

Go Home by Another Way

Scripture: The wise men go home a different way after seeing Jesus because of King Herod. (Matthew 2:1-12)

This Game Teaches: Sometimes people try to hurt Christians.

Materials: Twenty sheets of different colored paper that is 8 1/2 x 11, five stones

97

Game: Before you play the game, spread the twenty sheets of different colored paper on a playing area. Have the sheets fairly close together but not touching.

Say, "The wise men came to visit baby Jesus. As they started to go home, they realized that King Herod was trying to hurt baby Jesus, so they went home another way. We're going to play a game about the wise men avoiding King Herod."

Ask for a volunteer. Give the volunteer a rock. Have the volunteer place the rock on one of the pieces of paper. Say, "This rock is King Herod. We're going to play a game where you skip around the room. When I say, 'Home,' I want you to jump onto the nearest colored paper. If you happen to land on the paper with the rock on it, you're out because King Herod got you."

Play the game. After you say, "Home," once, ask for another volunteer to place a second rock on a second piece of paper. Play the game again.

Continue playing the game. Each time you say, "Home," add another rock.

End the game by having the children stand in a circle and hold hands. "Our church is another safe home. We come together to worship God and to be with other people who believe in God."

Drip, Drop, Flood

Scripture: The flood. (Genesis 7)
This Game Teaches: A little water is not a big deal, but a lot of water is.
Materials: A plastic cup, a water source, a warm or hot day to play outdoors

Game: Before you play this game, check with parents to make sure kids can get wet. Play this game outside on a warm or hot day.

Briefly tell the story about Noah's ark and the flood. Have the children sit in a circle. Ask for one child to be the volunteer.

Give the volunteer a plastic cup filled with water. Have the child walk around the circle and carefully pour one drop of water on

each child's head while saying, "drip." (This game is similar to Duck, Duck, Goose except that the child will say Drip, Drip, Flood.)

The volunteer will continue going around the circle until he or she decides to pour the rest of the contents of the cup onto one child's head while saying, "Flood." The child with the cup then starts to run around the circle while the drenched kid chases him or her.

Most likely the drenched child will not catch the volunteer because it's rather shocking to get doused with water and then get up and run to catch someone. So have the wet child be the next volunteer for the next game.

End the game by standing in a circle and shaking the water off like dogs.

Bonus Idea

Give each child a cup. Have a water source nearby. Have children walk around, dip their fingers into their cups and "drip" on other kids. When they feel ready, let kids "flood" each other periodically before refilling their cups.

All the People of the World

Scripture: God blesses everyone around the world. (Galatians 3:6-9)
This Game Teaches: Everyone in every country matters.
Materials: Four balloons, four chopsticks

Game: Before you play, inflate two balloons. (Keep the other two balloons for backup in case either balloon pops.)

Form two teams of an equal number of players. If you have an odd number of children, have one team choose one child who will go twice.

Have the children form two lines. Give the first child in each line a balloon and two chopsticks. Say, "Everyone in the world matters.

God blesses each and every one. We're going to play a game that emphasizes different people. First we'll have an Asian relay. Use the chopsticks to carry your balloon to this point and back." Designate a point. Place a chair or some other object to mark it.

Say, "When you return to your line, carefully hand off the chopsticks with the balloon inside of it to the next child who will then race with the balloon. If the balloon ever drops, stop. Pick it up, place it back between the chopsticks and continue."

Play the game. After the first race, repeat the game using these actions (one at a time):

- Bat the balloon into the air and say "Jambo" each time you hit it. ("Jambo" means hello in Swahili, which is the official language of East African countries, such as Tanzania and Kenya.)
- Place the balloon under your shirt like you're pregnant. Waddle with your toes pointed outward to the point and back.
- Hold the balloon high in the air as you walk to the point (to show that God blesses everyone who lives in high places) and then hold the balloon near the ground as you walk back (to show that God blesses everyone who lives in valleys).

End the game by asking the children for relay ideas. Close with prayer, "Thank you, God, for blessing each person on this earth. Amen."

Famous Animals in the Bible

Scripture: Jonah and the whale (Jonah 1-2), Daniel in the lion's den (Daniel 6), the Holy Spirit appears as a dove during Jesus' baptism (Luke 3), Jesus rides into Jerusalem on a donkey (Luke 19), and Jesus is the good shepherd of the sheep (John 10).
This Game Teaches: Children often know Bible stories because of the animals in them (and enjoy learning more about animals in the Bible).
Materials: Bibles, five pieces of paper, pen

100

Game: Before you play this game, write one of the scriptures above (along with the description) on a separate piece of paper. For example, the first piece of paper will say, "Jonah and the whale (Jonah 1-2)."

Have children gather together. Say, "The Bible is filled with famous animals. How many do you know?"

Ask for a volunteer. Let the volunteer choose one of the five pieces of paper. Without saying what is on the paper, the person needs to describe the animal to the

group. The rest of the children then need to guess the animal and which Bible story it is in.

When children have figured out the first one, ask for another volunteer. Repeat the game until all five pieces of paper have been used.

End the game by asking children if they know of other animals mentioned in the Bible. (You may be surprised.) Then end with a prayer, thanking God for all the animals. Have children make animal noises before you say, "Amen."

Bonus Idea

If you want children to learn more about animals in the Bible, adapt this game so that children use the Bible to look up passages to find out which animals appear in the story. Study passages such as Genesis 1:20-23 (on the fifth day, God created fish and birds), Genesis 1:24-25 (on the sixth day, God created all the land animals), Exodus 8:1-15 (the plague of the frogs), Exodus 8:16-19 (the plague of the gnats), Exodus 8:20-32 (the plague of the flies), Exodus 10:1-20 (the plague of the locusts), Exodus 31-32 (people made an idol that looked like a calf), Numbers 21 (snakes were biting people), 1 Kings 17 (birds brought food to Elijah), 2 Kings 2 (Elijah goes to heaven in a chariot made of fire), and John 6 (Jesus feeds the 5,000 with fish—along with loaves of bread).

A Bank of Thanks

Scripture: Be thankful. (Colossians 3:15-17)
This Game Teaches: Be thankful.
Materials: One or two rolls of pennies (each roll has fifty pennies, and you can get rolls of pennies from a bank), a jar, a whistle

Game: Place a jar in the middle of a playing area. Divide all the pennies between children who are present. Read aloud Colossians 3:15-17. Say, "We have much to be thankful for. We're going to play a game. We'll start out by skipping around the room. When I blow a whistle, stop. If I name a description that fits you, run to the thank bank and name one thing you're thankful for while dropping one coin into the bank."

Play the game. Periodically stop to name a category. Use categories such as these:

- Has black hair
- Has a sister
- Has brown eyes
- Wears tennis shoes
- Has something in a pocket
- Has blue eyes
- Has two feet
- Has a loose tooth
- Is hungry
- Has a brother
- Has a pet
- Knows words from a second language
- Can whistle
- Can write in cursive
- Is ticklish
- Has two eyes

End the game by having the children place any remaining coins into the thank bank. Explain that you will place all the money into your church offering. Then form a circle. Pass around the thank bank from child to child as each child names one more thing to be thankful for: what he or she likes best about your church.

Bonus Idea

With the children, create a thank bank to keep in your classroom. Maybe you could glue sequins and fake jewels (found in a craft store) to a jar. Or you could glue colored tissue paper to a jar. Encourage children to bring coins each time you meet and place coins in the thank bank while naming what they're thankful for. Place the money in your church's offering plate or give it to a local charity. If the idea catches on, have children each make their own thank bank and keep one at home.

Ten Keys to Making Great Games Even Better

A great game can become an even better game when you incorporate some key features while planning and playing the game. Consider these ten keys:

Key #1: Follow Kids' Interest

A great game will lose its impact if you play it too long. It's more strategic to cut a game short (and have kids begging for more) than to drag it out past its use.

Key #2: Play with the Kids

Children enjoy playing with their peers, but they also crave playtime with adults. Play with the kids. If you have other adult volunteers with you, get them in the game as well. Children will have more fun when you're engaged and they witness adults cutting loose.

Key #3: Stick with the Rules of the Game

Be clear about the game's rules, and stick with them throughout the game. (Some kids may try to change them.) Encourage children to ask questions when they don't understand rules. If anyone begins to bend the rules, stop the game and remind everyone of the rules. Games are more fun when everyone knows what to expect.

Key #4: Vary the Activity Level of the Games

Some games require more physical exertion. Others require more mental stimulation. Vary the games so that children aren't getting too tired doing too many physical games or too many intellectually stimulating games too close together.

Key #5: Enhance Your Curriculum with Games Whenever You Can

Most Christian education curricula do great in teaching a lesson, but many often lack physical activity. Use games from this book to add physical activity and more learning to your curriculum.

Key #6: Keep Competition to a Minimum

Although some of the games in this book have winners and losers, do not emphasize the competition. Instead, emphasize the fun of playing the game and how good it feels to try to play more strategically each time.

Key #7: Rotate the Leadership of Games

Many of these games require a volunteer or two. Make sure that everyone gets a chance to be a volunteer or a leader of a game. If you have a lot of children, keep track of your game leaders by posting them on a sheet on the wall.

Key #8: Experiment with the Age Levels of Games

Sometimes you may have a lot of younger children in your kindergarten to third-grade group. Try some of the preschool games and see how they respond. Or if you have a lot of third-graders, try a game or two from the fourth- to sixth-graders section.

Key #9: Keep Track of the Games Kids Love

Sometimes a new game does not go well the first time we play it and the kids become restless. Ask them which game they would like to play instead—even if it doesn't fit with your lesson. Sometimes a favorite game can rebuild children's enthusiasm so that the rest of your lesson goes smoother.

Key #10: Have Fun

The key to a great game is the fun factor. Follow the laughter. Follow the giggles. Have fun when you play together.

Looking for More Great Games?

101 Great Games for Kids by Jolene L. Roehlkepartain is the original games book that brought scripture to life by getting kids up and moving. Divided into four sections, *101 Great Games for Kids* includes easy-to-use games for preschoolers, children in grades K–3, children in grades 4–6, and groups of mixed-aged children. A scripture guide provides quick help in locating specific Bible passages.

101 Great Games for Infants, Toddlers, and Preschoolers by Jolene L. Roehlkepartain highlights creative ways to play with young children from birth to age five. Each game includes a scripture passage, a teaching point, a supervision tip, materials needs, and easy-to-use game instructions. Even as babies are beginning to crawl, toddlers are learning to speak, and preschoolers are starting to cooperate with playmates, they can begin to discover God's word and God's world through play.

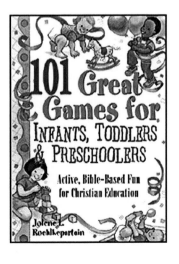

101 Great Games for Kids and *101 Great Games for Infants, Toddlers, and Preschoolers* are available from Abingdon Press, Nashville, Tennessee.

Scripture Index

New Testament

Topical Index

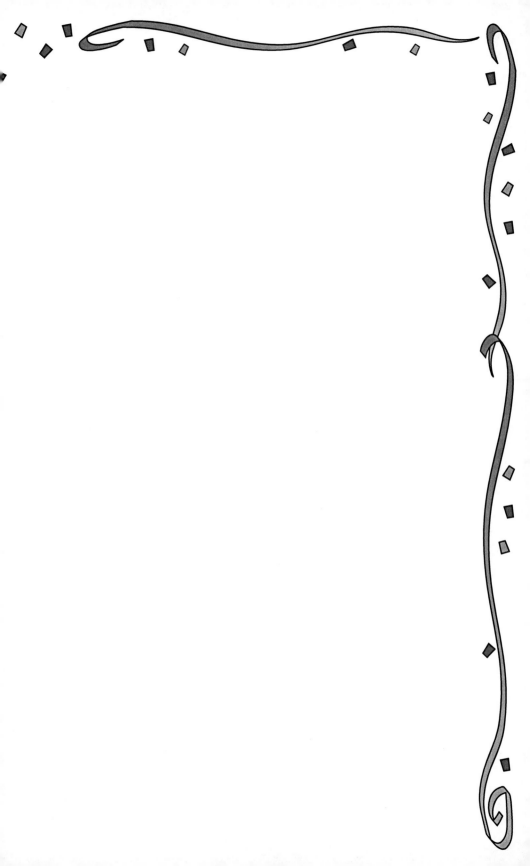

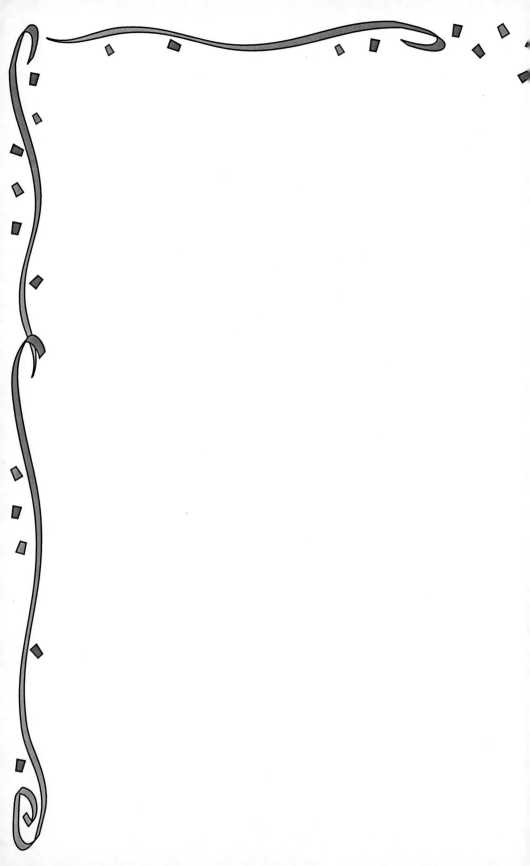

PPPJLGI

268.432
R713
2007

LINCOLN CHRISTIAN UNIVERSITY

126999

CPSIA information can be obtained at www.ICGtesting.com
Printed in the USA
LVOW101529050313

322834LV00020B/694/P

3 4711 00217 2973